You'd Better
Believe It!

Where You Spend Eternity
Depends Upon It!

by

Dr. Ernest DePasquale

(Scriptures taken from NKJV unless otherwise noted)
ISBN 978-1-884687-73-0
© 2007 Dr. Ernest DePasquale

Table of Contents

Dedication
Introduction

Dedication

This book is dedicated to the memory of a modern-day martyr, the late Watchman Nee, my Chinese spiritual mentor, through whose writings I have gained much understanding of the Scriptures and the plan of God. Much of his doctrine is included in this book.

I thank God for his life, which mirrored the life of St. Paul, since he set up over 700 churches in Communist China, and suffered much persecution for the sake of Jesus Christ. In fact, Watchman Nee was thrown into a Communist prison for many years where he died in 1972.

I owe him a great debt of gratitude for his unique ability to interpret Scripture, which conveyed to me a clear understanding of the Gospel, thus transforming my life.

INTRODUCTION

As a medical doctor for the past 27 years, my job has been to help people get well through sound medical advice, treatment, and medication. You might say that my life-long passion has simply been to *help* people – and at that time this was the best way I could think of to help them.

Only by the grace of God was I able to succeed – and in His generous outpouring, he caused me to do even more than succeed! I knew, even as a young man that, had I not learned to place my trust in God long before I became a doctor, it would never have come to pass. However, this long and toilsome road was made possible exclusively by trusting in God, for without His guidance I knew that I was incapable – in my own strength – to accomplish my goal.

Since that time, I find that there is an even greater goal than preserving the physical health of my patients: **They must face the fact that one day they are going to die – in spite of good medicine!** *Their greatest need is a spiritual one,* and, as a doctor, I can help heal people through medicine – but now my passion has broadened to see them healed for eternity! I have an obligation to see that this area is addressed as well.

This leads me to why I feel compelled to write this book. If they hope to fulfill their life's destiny, people need to believe in God – and more specifically, in His Son Jesus Christ. To that end I have endeavored to present a clear case for surrendering to His authority.

Why?

Because where they spend eternity
Depends upon it!
And that is *ultimate* healing!

Chapter One
IS THERE A GOD?

The world asks, "Is there a God?" Many argue that there is not. Many others argue that there is.

Well, let's look at the evidence. Let's start with nature, the world, and every phenomenon in it. The universe displays countless diverse forms, colors, shapes and textures. We can see these with our own eyes. The explanation for all these phenomena is known as "knowledge." Philosophers and all thoughtful people can only come up with two explanations as far as the origin of the universe is concerned. One says that it came into being through natural evolution and self-interaction; the second attributes its origin to a personified Being with wisdom, intellect and purpose. A third explanation does not exist.

How did the world come into existence? By itself, through *chance*? Or was it designed by a Creator from whom we derive the concept of God? First, let's list the characteristics of things that come about by chance. We know that they are unorganized. At most they can be partially integrated. They can never be totally organized. It's possible to achieve a specified goal by chance once, but never all the time. Anything that comes together by chance can only be integrated partially, never totally.

For example, if one were to throw a chair to the other side of a room, by chance it may land in the right spot. If this were repeated with a second chair, by chance, it may also settle neatly beside the first one. But this will not continue with subsequent throws. *Chance* can only provide partial organization. It does not guarantee total integration. Besides, all random interactions are aimless, disorganized, and purposeless. Without order and structure, they are loose, formless, disorderly, and cannot be trusted to perform. Basically, the characteristics of chance events are disharmony, irregularity, inconsistency, and insignificance.

Really, this pretty well describes Genesis 1:2, (NAS) where this earth is described. *"And the earth was formless and void, and darkness was over the surface of the deep."* Now look at the world today. Vast mountain ranges, waves crashing on ocean beaches, thundering waterfalls, wooded dells, and sunshine warmth on a winter's day. Now I ask you, can anyone honestly believe that these *just happened?*

While you're thinking about that, let's examine another marvel: a human being! A baby is carried in its mother's womb for nine months and delivered. The child has ten fingers – no more (unless there is a genetic defect). Two eyes and two ears spaced according to the design. There is one nose and one mouth. Humans all over the world are designed like that. Humans grow up, reproduce after their kind, live some 70 or 80 years, and eventually die. This cycle is repeated for every single individual. Consistent. Trustworthy. A human being does not evolve from a wild game of chance.

What about the NASA space program? When the astronomers send up a shuttle, they must know where the celestial bodies are so the shuttle doesn't run into them. What if they just floated haphazardly here and there? What holds them in orbit?

All these show that the universe – which is so vast that not even the Hubble telescope can see it all – is organized, consistent, and purposeful. Even when a blade of grass or a flower petal is viewed under a microscope, one can observe their meticulously rhythmic and finely-fashioned structure. Nothing is disorganized or confused. Everything is disciplined and functional. One fact comes out of all of this: the universe, and everything in it, has purpose and meaning.

There are people who are so bold as to say that there is no God in the universe, but I personally do not know anyone. But setting this question aside for the time being, let us consider the universe again. It is enormous, beyond our finite ability to imagine, but at the same time, it is very small. Objects that are even undetectable to the microscope have definite structures, laws, and order. This is true of every microscopic object you consider. It used to be said that atoms were the smallest objects. Later, it was discovered that electrons were even smaller. Recently, men have found that there are particles even smaller than electrons. Although these particles are small, they have definite laws, principles, and order governing them. Now, think about this: *If there is no God, who is organizing these things? How can they result from coincidence?* There must be a God who rules and arranges everything. Otherwise, how can we have the awesome order that we have in the world today? This can only speak of two possibilities: Either it was by chance, or Someone set it into place. Either Someone has arranged these things, or they have come about by accident.

Anything that happens by chance happens without a reason; anything by arrangement speaks of Someone behind the scene who is planning and executing his or her will. To illustrate, let's take a bicycle – brand new, unassembled, in a box. Many of us have put together a bicycle – you know how it goes – the frame, handlebars, wheels, chain, and seat, along with a few nuts and bolts. For those who say the universe came about by chance, let's say that two people picked up this box and shook it over and over again, day after day, month after month, even year after year? Would a bicycle ever form? Could this bicycle ever be produced by chance? No, of course not.

Ask yourself, "Then how could the vast universe have been produced by chance?" An experienced carpenter might make a wooden chair in a half hour. But if we waited for it to be produced by chance, we'd still be sitting on the ground! No, when you consider the expanse of the universe, no thinking person could be duped into thinking it could have come about by chance. Someone had to design the universe for it to be as orderly and logical as it is. Even a fool can come to this conclusion.

As the Scripture says, ***"The fool hath said in his heart, "There is no God."*** (Psalm 14:1·) That's putting it pretty plain! But I didn't say it! God did.

Therefore, I am convinced that the universe has a Creator – God – who by His profound wisdom, vast knowledge, and intricate design formed our world. Only a God who is all-wise, all-encompassing, and all-powerful could have brought it to pass. Realizing that random formation of the universe is impossible, mankind will have to admit that it was created by an awesome God! There cannot be a third explanation.

The choice is yours. If you're a betting person, would you gamble on "chance," or would you bet on "God?"

Chapter Two
RELIGION

The word "religion" is usually used with regard to spiritual disciplines. *Webster's New World Dictionary* describes it as "any system of beliefs, practices and ethical values." Therefore, we need to understand that the word "religion" takes many forms. For instance, one may brush their teeth "religiously!" In this connotation, "religion" becomes nothing more than a *conscientious habit!*

For our purposes, then, let me propose that there are two kinds of spiritual "religion:" one based on natural concepts (human ideology) and the other based on God's revelation to mankind.

"Natural" religion starts with man as the center. He is the one seeking to appease God. But, "revelational" religion comes directly from God Almighty. *He* is the One who comes to reveal Truth to us through His prophets and apostles as found in His inspired, written Word, the Bible. Man's thoughts are often vain imaginations. God's revelation alone is trustworthy.

Christianity is different from all other "natural" religions in that it comes from Divine revelation. Christianity begins with God. It is God who comes to seek out man, rather than man who first seeks after God. Assuming that God wants to reveal Himself to man and fellowship with Him, He must do it through human means. Therefore, He sent His Son Jesus, born of a woman, by the power of the Holy Spirit, who became fully human and walked among us. Note that Jesus often referred to Himself as "the Son of Man." (Matthew 8:20) In addition, God manifests Himself through the written Word or the spoken Word by revelation of the Holy Spirit.

Various religions have their "holy books." Christians have the Bible. In it, God reveals Himself through the written Word, and Christians believe it is Divinely inspired. Volumes have been written by different people throughout the centuries, describing their beliefs to which they adhere, and these books have produced some of the world's most powerful religions. It is important to test these systems of belief. Such a book must prove not only the existence of that god, but it must contain his written revelations as well.

Our God has one Book in this universe, and we test it by making certain it meets specific conditions and has certain qualifications before one can say it is from God.

(1) It first of all must tell us that it is from God and that God is its author.

(2) Second, it must have a moral goal that is impossible to reach by human efforts.

(3) Third, this Divine Book must describe information about both the past and the future of this world, which is known exclusively by God. Further, predictions in the form of prophecy must stand the test of time and come to pass.

(4) Fourth, this book must be readable and available so that everyone may be able to have and understand it. It cannot be a "secret" writing for only a few adherents.

There have been several important writings throughout human history, but only one meets all these requirements and we set forth the premise that the Holy Bible is that Book.

To be fair, let us compare some other "holy books."

India's book is called the *Rig-Veda*. It once dominated Hinduism, but it does not claim to be written by God.

Next, Buddhism is a religion that is void of a deity. Its founder, Sakya Muni, did not believe in the existence of God.

In the Middle East there is a book called the *Avesta*, written by a Persian named Zoroaster. It is also very influential, but its moral overtone is far from commendable.

In China, there is Confucius. If you read his books, you will find he did conduct a moral and proper life. But he never claimed to be God, either. Hence, he fails the first step.

Finally, there is the *Koran*, Islam's book of Mohammedanism. This comes the closest in meeting all the quailfications. It tells us that it comes from God, thereby meeting the first requirement. However, it does not fulfill the second requirement, for its moral tone is too sensual. The heaven it describes is full of lust of the flesh, and rather than condemning them for this, its adherents are urged to aspire to its delights. Our Holy God could never condone such licentiousness and immorality. Indeed, God chastised such behavior wherever He found it throughout the Scriptures. Therefore, the *Koran* does not pass the test of morality.

Thus, after researching all the "holy" books, we find that only the Bible passes all four tests. In the Old Testament, the words, "Thus saith the Lord," appear over 1,000 times. You might put it this way: "This is God speaking." In the New Testament there are over 2,000 references attributed to God which claim they are of Divine origin.

Next, moving on to the second qualification, everyone who has studied this Book admits that it carries the highest moral standard. Even the sins of the most saintly individuals are recorded and condemned without mercy! The human idea is that all sexual acts outside of marriage are considered as sin (fornication). The Bible, however, says that *even an evil thought* is fornication. (Matthew 5:27-28) The human psyche condemns an act of killing as murder, but the Bible condemns *anger at one's brother* as murder. (Matthew 5:22) People consider a man who lets his enemy get away without taking revenge as being *forgiving*. But the Bible commands that we "love" our enemy. Therefore, we can see the extremely high moral tone of the Bible, and how far short we fall of its standards.

The Bible also describes in detail the past, present, and future of the universe. The books of **Genesis** and **The Revelation** portray the origin and destiny of the heavens and the earth, respectively. No other "holy" book has done that. In the Bible, past conditions of the world and its future destiny are both recorded; therefore, the third qualification is also met.

Finally, the last qualification states that it must be available to the masses. What is the circulation of this great Book? In the last 40 years alone the eight new Bible versions published in English have sold well in excess of 100,000,000 copies! This does not include the millions published and sold yearly in other languages throughout the world. Furthermore, this Book has been translated into more than 720 languages – and more are being translated as we write! The American Bible Society and the Wycliffe translators are endeavoring to get the Word written in every language in every country, and among every race, until the last remote tribe has been reached with a translation of this unique Book.

So far, it is extremely easy for anyone to obtain a Bible in the United States. However, it is still a scarce commodity in many persecuted places in this world, such as India. The Bible is without doubt the world's bestselling Book. When added together, the number of Bibles produced throughout the world far exceeds anything printed and published in the history of mankind.

Chapter Three
THE BIBLE

From the foregoing, we can see that the Bible is truly the inspired Word of God, His revelation to mankind. God's omnipotent hand is behind the more than 30 people of different backgrounds and ideas in different times and places, whose writings comprise its 66 books. Yet, when put together, they harmonize as though they were written by one individual! Genesis was written about 1500 years before Christ, and The Revelation was written 95 years *after* Him. Between the first and last books of the Bible, there is a time span of 1600 years! Whatever begins in Genesis is concluded in The Revelation. This amazing feature cannot be explained in human terms. Every word of it has to be written by God – *through* man. God is the motivating One behind the whole composition. Paul wrote this about the Bible: *"All scripture is given by inspiration of God...."* (2 Timothy 3:16) The prophet Isaiah recognized the indestructibility of the Word when he declared: *"The grass withers the flower fades, but the word of God stands forever."* (Isaiah 40:8)

Now, in this wonderful Book, what is God's underlying message to all mankind? The central theme of the entire Bible is Jesus Christ! The meaning of "Jesus" is "God the Savior" or "Jehovah Savior." "Christ" is a Greek word meaning "the Anointed One." It is the same as the Hebrew word "Messiah." The Old Testament looked forward in time to the coming of Jesus Christ: *"Then He said to them, 'These are the words which I spoke to you while I was still with you, that all things must be fulfilled which were written in the Law of Moses and the Prophets and the*

Psalms concerning Me.'" (Luke 24:44) The New Testament looks back to Jesus Christ, and both look forward to the promise of His future return.

The theme of the Old Testament is: God created, Satan damaged, man fell, and God promised the coming of Christ for redemption (meaning to "recover, ransom or rescue"). Although there are 39 books in the Old Testament, it mainly shows us that God created the universe, Satan came in to damage God's creation, man fell, and God promised the coming of Christ for accomplishment of redemption. Therefore, the Christ in the Old Testament was only a *hope* for man, because He was only promised by God to fallen man as the Messiah, the Redeemer.

The theme of the New Testament is how Christ came to redeem sinners and establish His Church according to God's plan. In it we see how Christ builds up His glorious Church as His mystical Body for God to have an entity through which to express Himself.

What is God's purpose and plan as revealed in the Bible? The Apostle Paul tells us that, *"According to the eternal purpose which He accomplished in Christ Jesus our Lord...."* (Ephesians 3:11) This plan is the mystery of His will. *"Having made known to us the mystery of His will, according to His good pleasure which He purposed in Himself...."* (Ephesians 1:9) This mystery is something unknown to man. God's eternal will is that all things in the heavens and on earth be headed up in Christ. *"That in the dispensation of the fullness of the times He might gather together in one all things in Christ, both which are in heaven and which are on earth – in Him...."* (Ephesians 1:10) In other words, Christ is to be the Head over all things. When this happens, everything in the universe will express the Lord. This is God's eternal will.

The book of Hebrews tells us that long ago God spoke many times and in many ways to our ancestors through the prophets. But now in these final days, He has spoken to us through His Son. God promised everything to the Son as an inheritance, and through the Son He made the universe and everything in it. *"All things came into being through Him; and apart from Him nothing came into being that has come into being."* (John 1:3)

The Son reflects His Father's own glory, and everything about Him represents God exactly. *"Who being the brightness of His glory and the express image of His person, and upholding all things by the word of His power, when he had by himself purged our sins, sat down at the right hand of the Majesty on High."* (Hebrews 1:3) Jesus sustains the universe by the mighty power of His command! After He died to cleanse us from every stain of sin, He sat down in the place of honor at the right hand of the majestic God of Heaven! This shows that God's Son is far greater than the angels, just as the name God gave Him, Jesus Christ, is far greater than their names. *"For to which of the angels did He ever say: 'You are My Son, today I have begotten You?' And again: 'I will be to Him a Father, and He shall be to Me a Son?'"* (Hebrews 1:5)

Christ is the key to all Truth. He is central to understanding His Word. Without Him the Bible would be a dead book. Without Him we would never understand the Scriptures. Therefore, when we are confronted with difficult passages in God's Word, we can relate them to Christ, who will enlighten our understanding.

The Bible centers upon just One Person – the Lord Jesus Christ. He Himself declares*: "Ye search the scriptures ... and these are they that bear witness of me."* (John 5:39) This is likewise confirmed by these words of the Lord: *"In the roll of the book it is written of me...."* (Hebrews 10:7) The Bible is the written Word of God, and Christ is the living Word of God. The written Word bears witness to the living Word, while the living Word fulfills the written Word.

Lastly, I like to think of the Bible described this way:

BIBLE – **B**asic **I**nstructions **B**efore **L**eaving **E**arth!

Chapter Four
GOD BECOMING MAN

So far we've discussed the subjects, "Is There a God?", "Religion," and "The Bible" and we have seen how God continues to reveal Himself through His *written* Word. Now we will examine His revelation through the *spoken* Word.

Full understanding of someone cannot be achieved merely through writing. Think of two lovers, conducting their courtship from one continent to another by mail. Their letters would be full of endearing words, promises of eternal love, longing to be together, and hardly able to wait until the day they meet at the airport with wild demonstrations of love! After all the time of waiting, now they can see with their eyes, hear with their ears, and touch. Direct contact is a hundred times more fulfilling!

Likewise, how could God accomplish such a task when fallen mankind cannot see a Spirit or communicate with Him – even though God's heart is full of love and desires to have an intimacy with us such as He had with Adam and Eve – especially after that man, Adam, disobeyed and cut mankind off from his Heavenly Father.

So if God's intention is to reveal Himself to us, He must of necessity do so through speaking, but how? If God remained God, we could never understand Him. It would be worse than a man trying to communicate with an ant. If God wants to reveal Himself through speaking and have fellowship with man, He must *reduce Himself* to such a degree that He actually becomes one of us! Only then would He be able to speak our language and tell us of Himself and of the mysteries of the universe. Only then would we be able to understand Him.

Think of that! Has such a thing ever happened? Imagine the implications here, for they are *tremendous! What if God became a man and fellowshipped with humans?* It would mean that in this world, among all people throughout history, one person was not merely a man, but God as well! If it is true that God became a man, there must be a mortal who was also Divine. We need to find out about this One. Here again, there are certain qualifications a person must have if he is God.

(1) The first condition that this person must fulfill is that he must claim to be God while he is on earth. He must declare boldly that he is God. Only then can we know who he is. Therefore, such a declaration is the first qualification.

(2) The second condition: the way this person came into the world must be different from ours. If he said that he was God and yet was born in the same manner as every other human being, his words would be hollow. If, on the other hand, he came down from Heaven, his claim would have to be taken seriously.

(3) Third, this man must exhibit a moral standard that is far above that of all other human beings. He must have God's holiness and live a life of God's righteousness. If God is to become a man, His moral behavior must be of the highest quality. This is the only way that we could identify Him as "God." No "god" worth worshipping would disobey his own word.

(4) Fourth, if a person is God, he must be able to perform things which no mortal can do. He must achieve what we cannot do, as well as know all about everything in this world and the next. In truth, he must be able to perform *miracles* before we can say that he is truly God.

(5) Finally, this person must be able to explain the Divine purpose concerning mankind. What was God's purpose in creating the universe and man? How does He minister to man's pains and sorrows? What is the origin and ultimate solution of everything in the universe? What

attitude toward himself does He require of us? If any god is incapable of showing us what we do not see, he has no revelation for us.

Now, let us set down these five conditions and put the whole of humanity to the test. We will find out if anyone meets the five requirements and thereby qualifies to be God.

(1) The first person to put to the test should be yourself. You are not God, of course, because you have never claimed to be God. Therefore, you fail the first step.

(2) The next person we will examine is Sakya Muni, the founder of Buddhism. Not only was there an absence of the claim of divinity, but his philosophy itself is void of a god. He did not believe in the existence of any god. Since he had no god, he cannot be God, either.

(3) Moving on to Mohammed, we find that he believed in God – but he never claimed to be God. He called his God "Allah" and himself "the prophet of Allah."

If you check out every person in history, you will discover that no one ever claimed to be God except One – Jesus of Nazareth (unless he was a lunatic or a liar!). He claimed to be "the living God." Except for Jesus Christ, no other person in history has ever put forth such a claim.

In John 10:37-38, Jesus said, *"If I do not do the works of My Father, do not believe Me; but if I do them, even if you do not believe Me, believe the works so that you may come to know and continue to know...."* Know *what?* Watch this, because the following sentence is crucial: *"...that the Father is in Me and I am in the Father."* Who then *is* this man? He said that "He was in God" and "God was in Him!"

There are numerous passages like this one in the Bible. Another important one is also found in John, Chapter 14, Verses 6-7: *"Jesus said to him, I am the way and the truth and the life; no one comes to the Father except through Me. If you had known Me, you would have known My Father also; and henceforth you know Him and have seen Him."* It says clearly that if you know Jesus of Nazareth, you have known the invisible God! How can this be? It is because *He is God.*

Let's check this out. As we stated in the second condition, if God is to become a man, he must be born into the world in some way that is different from all other mortals, or he would just be an ordinary human. We come into the world through the birth portal from our parents, and are conceived by our mothers. To prove whether Jesus of Nazareth is an ordinary person or the incarnated God, we need to examine His birth. If His birth was not different from ours, we have to conclude that He was nothing but a man. If he is indeed God, he must have been born in some extraordinary manner.

If we study the birth of Jesus, we will find that it was very different from ours. First of all, He was born of a virgin. Both the Gospel of Matthew and the Gospel of Luke in the New Testament tell us this fact. Now, anyone who knows anything about human birth knows that this cannot happen! As a doctor, I can assure you of that fact! Yet, according to reliable sources, Jesus was born of a *virgin* whose name was Mary. There is enough Scripture to back this up without question.

This important fact enables us to conclude that He is not an ordinary person, and justifies our belief in His Divinity, and we can become Christians, knowing this is truth. But man's natural understanding cannot readily accept this fact. Modernistic theologians contend that one reason alone is enough to disprove the virgin birth – the event is biologically impossible. People deny the possibility of such an event based on biological law.

The question is asked, "Has this ever happened?" This question points to an historical occurrence. It is one thing to be academically accurate. It is another thing to be historically recorded.

Take for example this true story written in a newspaper not long ago: In the paper was an article about an accident that had happened a few days earlier. A man was driving on a winding mountain road. Due to his carelessness, the car slid off the road and tumbled down a deep, thousand-foot gorge. The car was totally demolished. Not even a square foot of the vehicle was left intact. It was without a doubt unrecognizably totaled – but the man on the ground was absolutely unhurt! Later, he got up, walked away, and was perfectly fine.

People could ask, "Could this man possibly live after such a wreck?" But the real question is, "Is this man alive?" The answer is, "Yes, *he is alive!*" In the natural, if anyone considers the possibility, there is none. But, *the fact is – he lived!*

The virgin birth is an historical fact. If studied from a scientific point of view, it may be concluded that this is an impossible event. But the question is, "Did such an event occur?" The Gospel of Matthew says that "Jesus was born of a virgin." (Matthew 1:18-25) So, also, does the Gospel of Luke. (Luke 1:26-28) The least that can be said is that these Gospels have said so, and that this event was recorded in history. The least one can do is to believe that there was an historical event. An historical event, indeed, Divinely inspired by the Holy Spirit!

The third qualification concerns morality. What morals did Jesus exhibit? Did He ever sin? In the Book of John, Chapter 8, Verse 46, Jesus was surrounded and cross-examined by the Jews, many of whom were opposing Him.

In return, Jesus asked, *"Which of you convicts Me of sin?"*

This was an awesome challenge! Who in the history of the world would dare to stand before everyone and challenge himself to be convicted of sin? But when Jesus made such a statement, no one was able to utter a word of rebuke! There have been a countless number of saints throughout the ages, but none was bold enough to claim to be perfect and sinless.

Therefore, Jesus is sinless. When He made such a statement, He made it before His enemies. If there had been the slightest misconduct on His part, the Jews would have leaped upon Him without mercy! After Jesus, many books were written by the Jews to contradict Him. All these books deny His Divinity, but none can touch His morality. Of all the opposing writings, none can prove that Jesus ever sinned – the controversial book, *The Da Vinci Code,* notwithstanding!

The fourth qualification is that one who claims to be God Incarnate must be able to perform what an ordinary person cannot. Jesus, indeed, performed numerous supernatural acts (miracles), as recorded in the New Testament. John 7:31 says, ***"But many out of the crowd believed on Him and said, Will the Christ, when He comes, do more signs than this man has done?"*** Many people testified that He performed all kinds of miracles which no man could do.

People today are not His contemporaries; He walked on earth 2000 years ago. Obviously, we cannot be His witnesses of what happened back then. But one thing is for certain: the apostles who followed Jesus recorded, preached, and testified the things concerning Him. The four Gospels were all completed within 30 years after His departure. Most of the Jews who were then alive had seen Jesus. If the apostles' records were false, they would have been repudiated long ago. However, the Jews only argued that Jesus is not the Son of God. They never denied His deeds and miracles, for they were all facts.

Today, when one reads the four Gospels, there is no doubt about their authenticity. If there had been the slightest error when they were written, there would have been serious problems, because many of the contemporaries had actually seen and heard Jesus. There was no chance for any fabrication. Therefore, these books cannot be a hoax. If the Jews could not attack these books back then, there is even less basis for an attack today.

The fifth qualification is best summed up in the Book of Matthew, Chapter 11, Verses 27-28: *"All things have been delivered unto me of my Father: and no one knoweth the Son, save the Father."* (Verse 27a) This tells us that the Son of God is a mystery, and "if" the Father reveals Him to us, then we know Him. This is by God's grace only, and it is called "the gift of faith." If God does not reveal Him to us we will not know Him. Before you are shown, however, the Lord is a mystery to you. If you read this from an objective standpoint, you will see the Lord as the Son of God, and you will worship Him. Otherwise, subjectively speaking, you will consider Him to be insane, for who can say such words?

"Neither doth any know the Father, save the Son, and he to whomsoever the Son willeth to reveal him." (Verse 27b) This is also a very powerful statement.

Reading this statement as an unbeliever, one could only say that Jesus is the Son of God. The Lord in this verse is pointing people to know the Father. Therefore, He must be the Son. If He were not God the Son He would not be able to lead us to know the Father. Now the Father knows Him, and He leads us to know the Father. Since the Father has delivered all things into His hand (Verse 27a), salvation, too, is in His hand. The Gentiles as well as the Jews are all in His hand. All men, in fact, are in His hand. For this reason He is able to say what is found in the next verse: *"Come unto me, all ye that labor and are heavy laden, and I will give you rest."* (Verse 28) Since all things have been delivered to Him (Verse 27a), He can now invite all men to come to Him.

So, it is clear that God has two means whereby He communicates with us: the written Word and the spoken language. For this reason, the Bible and Jesus are the two indispensable factors in our faith.

Hebrews 1:1 says, *"God, having spoken of old in many portions and in many ways to the fathers in the prophets...."* (these, His Words, make up the Bible) *"...has at the last of these days spoken to us in the Son."* (Verse 2) – this is Jesus of Nazareth.)

To sum up this chapter, I believe we must agree that to have heard the Words of Jesus is to have heard the Words of God!

Chapter Five
GOD'S PLAN

Try to picture this: Before He undertook the foundation of the world, God decided that the world would also "love the Son." John 17:24 tells us that the Father loved the Son "*...before the foundation of the world.*" The second thing that God purposed before the foundation of the world was to "foreordain His Son to be the Christ (or 'the anointed One')." 1 Peter 1:20 says that *"...before the foundation of the world...."* God foreordained the Son to be the Christ.

Now, this plan was good, but it gets better! Ephesians 1:4-5 also tells us that God "chose us" in Christ and predestinated us "unto sonship" (whereby we become God's sons, also in Christ) before the foundation of the world! *Not only did God foreordain the Son to be the Christ, He also chose us in Christ and predestinated us unto sonship!* Is this not evidence of God's supreme love for mankind?

2 Timothy 1:9 says that God gave us grace "before the times of the ages." Titus 1:2 also tells us that God promised us eternal life "before the times of the ages." Understand that He promised us that we would *participate in His life!* These two verses tell us that in order to receive the sonship, God predestinated us unto grace and life. So all of these things were purposed by God before the foundation of the world.

So why did God choose to create man? Genesis 1:26-27 tells us (and these two verses are extremely important): *"Let Us make man in Our image, according to Our likeness; let them have dominion over the fish of the sea, and birds of the air, and over the cattle, and over all the earth, and over every creeping thing that creeps on the earth. So God created man in His Own image; in the image of God He created him; male and female He created them."*

The creation of man was more special than all of God's other creations; consequently it required a council of the Godhead (God the Father, God the Son, and God the Holy Spirit). That Divine council agreed and said, *"Let us...."* This phrase is plural and reveals the fact that there was discussion and consultation in the Godhead, and together They laid out the blueprint for the creation of man.

Note here these spectacular words: *"Let Us make man in Our image, according to Our likeness."*(Verse 26) But Verse 27 tells us that *"...God created him in His own image; in the image of God He created him; male and female He created them."* In Verse 26 the word "Us" signifies plurality, but in Verse 27, the word "His" is singular in number. Grammatically speaking, if the phrase, *"Let Us make man in Our image"* in Verse 26 reveals a consultation among the Father, Son and Holy Spirit of the Godhead, then Verse 27 should have similarly read: "So God created man in 'their' image ... male and female created 'they' them."!

Why this apparent discrepancy? I believe it is because the Godhead has only One who has an *image,* and that One is *the Son.* For this reason, at the consultation of the Godhead, this Divine utterance came forth: "Let Us make man in Our image" (for They are One), but in describing the actual creation of man the Bible declared: "...in His image." This shows us that Adam was created in the image of the Lord Jesus. It wasn't the other way around, where first Adam was created, then later the Lord Jesus came in his image. When God created Adam He created him in the image of the Lord Jesus. That is why it is written: "...in His image" and not "...in Their image."

God's work has a definite goal in mind: That our labor should be correlated with His goal, which is the centrality and universality (not limited by time and space) of

Christr *"...that in all things He might have the pre-eminence...."* (Colossians 1:18) Christ is not only the Christ of the Jews and the Christ of the Church, He is the Christ of all things. *"The mystery of God, even Christ...."* (Colossians 2:2). Christ is the Head; therefore He includes all. And the death of Christ is an all-inclusive death. Just as Christ has died, so also all things included in the Head died also. Christ's death as Head had brought all things as well as mankind into death, thus reconciling all things and mankind back to God.

"Thou art the Christ, the Son of the living God...." (Matthew 11:16) *"For we preach ... Christ Jesus as Lord...."* (2 Corinthians 4:5) This means that Christ is the centrality of God. He is the thread that is woven throughout the Bible and in all the truths of God. Paul revealed that Jesus was *"...The mystery of God, even Christ."* A mystery is something that is hidden and this truth was hidden for eons in God's heart. Think about this! Never before had God told anyone why He created all things, including mankind. It remained a mystery for a long time, until God revealed this mystery to the Apostle Paul so that he might explain it. And this mystery, explained Paul, is Christ.

So let us review this once again with some added detail. God conceived an eternal plan before the foundation of the world. His plan, as we have said, serves the dual purpose of (1) having all things manifest Christ, and (2) conforming man into the image of Christ – which is to say, for man to have the life and glory of Christ. In realizing His dual aim, God encountered two problems: (1) the rebellion of Satan, and (2) the fall of man.

In an earlier age an archangel became jealous, through pride, at seeing Christ as the center of all things. (Isaiah 14:12-14) He wished to exalt himself to be equal with the Son of God. Intent on grasping for himself the centrality of Christ, he rebelled. One third of the angelic hosts followed him in rebellion against God. Even the living creatures on earth followed suit. Satan's rebellion hurled all things into chaos; it no longer being possible for them to manifest Christ. All things today may still declare the glory of God (Psalm 19:1), but they certainly cannot manifest God Himself.

God therefore created man in order that (1) having the life and glory of Christ and being given dominion over all things, man might bring all things back to God; and (2) being united with God, he might be used of Him to deal with Satan's rebellion. Unfortunately, man fell.

Therefore, for God's dual purpose to be realized, He must now resolve these two problems. He must (1) redeem fallen mankind, and (2) eliminate Satan's rebellion.

In order to realize God's dual purpose and resolve God's two problems, the Lord Jesus came down from Heaven to become man and accomplish the work of redemption. He is the Christ of all things as well as the Christ of mankind. He is the centrality as well as the universality. "Universality" means "that which is not limited by time and space." As we said earlier, Christ is not only the Christ of the Jews and the Christ of the Church, He is the Christ of all things. He is all, and in all.

The redemption of Christ has three cardinal features:

(1) Substitution - for the individual
(2) Representation - for the church
(3) Headship - for all things

Christ is the Head, therefore He includes all things. And the death of Christ is an all-inclusive death. So, just as Christ as Head died, so all things included in Him died, too. His death as the "Head" has brought all things as well as mankind into death, thus reconciling all things and mankind back to God.

On the Cross, Christ resolved every problem. There, He crushed the head of the serpent. He solved the problem of Satan's rebellion and destroyed all of Satan's works. There, too, He redeemed fallen mankind and reconciled all things back to God. Through the Cross, He imparts His life to men that they may be "conformed to His image."

Hallelujah! The Cross has accomplished Christ's double purpose and resolved God's two great problems!

Chapter Six
GOD'S PURPOSE

From the beginning, God planned to have a man who could rule over His earth. God wasn't looking for a robot; He wanted a man with a free will who wanted to love and obey Him. But man, through his disobedience, failed to accomplish this. Romans 5:19 tells us: ***"Through the one man's disobedience the many were made sinners."***

How were we made sinners? We aren't left in the dark about this! It's clear that it was through Adam's disobedience. We do not become sinners by what we *do*, but because of what Adam *did*. By Adam's Fall, a fundamental change took place in the character of Adam. That day (as warned by God) Adam died spiritually, whereby he became a sinner – one constitutionally unable to please God. We all share this family likeness, inwardly and outwardly, exhibiting his sinful character. Because of this, we have been "constituted sinners." How? ***"By the disobedience of one,"*** says the Apostle Paul. And so we are all sinners – members of a human family who are constitutionally other than what God intended us to be.

Let's face it. We are sinners, not because of ourselves but because of Adam. It is not because I individually have sinned that I am a sinner, but because I was in Adam when *he* sinned. Because by birth I descend from Adam, therefore I am a part of him. Furthermore, I can do nothing to alter this. I cannot, by improving my behavior, make myself other than a part of Adam, and, therefore, a sinner. The Bible's view of the Fall of mankind says that due to the unity of men, when the first man Adam sinned, all sinned in him, although as yet none had been born.

There is oneness of human life. Our life comes from Adam. Think, if your great-grandfather had died at the age of three, where would you be? You would have died in him! Your experience is bound up with his. And in just the same way, the experience of every one of us is bound up with that of Adam. None can say, "I have not been in the Garden of Eden," for potentially we all were there when Adam yielded to the serpent's words.

So we are all involved in Adam's sin, and by being born "in Adam" we receive from him all that he became as a result of his sin – that is to say, the Adam-nature which is the nature of a sinner. We derive our existence from him. Then, since he became sinful due to his fallen nature, the life which we inherit from him is also full of sin.

So, as we have said, the trouble is in our heredity, not in our behavior. Unless we can change our parentage there is no deliverance for us. But it is in this very direction that we shall find the solution of our problem, for that is exactly how God dealt with it – the Divine way of deliverance, which is Jesus Christ's death on the Cross and His resurrection from the dead! Who, but God, could have come up with such a Plan!

Not everyone born into this world is a child of God, for all humans are born in "original sin" inherited from Adam. Before we can become Sons of God, we must first be "reborn" (regenerated); that is, we must be born of God. Although not all the people in the world are yet the Sons of God, they *could* be! This is what redemption is all about! It all depends upon their desire and willingness! God gives the invitation, and we can choose life in Christ, where we will rule and reign with Him forever! Or – fools! – we can turn down the offer and choose to follow Satan to our great loss.

We had no choice as to who our parents would be. This is beyond man's control. We cannot choose our parents; yet the marvelous grace of God is so great that if a man decides to choose to become a Son of God, he can attain it!

Although he cannot regenerate *himself*, yet he can believe in the accomplished work of Jesus Christ's sacrificial death on the Cross and His resurrection from the dead. In return, God regenerates him, and he becomes a Son of God! Is that a great deal or not?

"For you are all Sons of God through faith in Christ Jesus." (Galatians 3:26) God's way is so simple! If one sees the danger of being Satan's child and the calamities that are to come, wisdom would tell him to become a Son of God and live. He only needs to believe in the testimony of God concerning His Son, Jesus Christ. He must trust in Him wholeheartedly, obey Him, accept Him as Savior by faith, and believe in the effectiveness of the salvation which Jesus accomplished on the Cross. By faith he can offer Jesus Christ up as the sinner's sin offering instead of the Old Testament unblemished lamb or bullock.

At that point, God will instantly forgive his sins, justify him, put a "new life" in him, and cause him to become a new creature in Christ Jesus! He will immediately become a Son of God. To believe in Christ Jesus is simply to *accept* the Lord Jesus as Savior.

"But as many as received Him, to them He gave the authority to become children of God, to those who believe into His name, who were begotten not of blood, nor the will of the flesh, nor of the will of man, but of God." (John 1:12-13)

God's grace is available for anyone who will accept it! What more could God do to bridge the gap between a Holy God and sinful man? It doesn't get any easier than this! In that split second of time when one receives the Lord Jesus as Savior and trusts in His accomplished salvation, that one has the authority to become the child of God. Because Christ has taken away the sins of the world, those who believe in Him are forgiven of their sins and are delivered from the punishment of sin. Once the problem of sin is solved, nothing can hinder those who believe in Him from receiving grace and truth. Once past sins have been dealt with, the Holy Spirit of God will pour God's life and nature into the hearts of those who believe in Him. Once they have the life of God within, they will instantly become the Sons of God. Regeneration happens at the moment when the life of God enters into their hearts. The work of regeneration is altogether the work of God.

Remember, the death of the Lord Jesus is inclusive. So the resurrection of the Lord Jesus is likewise inclusive. Try this. Think of yourself as a bookmark. It is in a book. Wherever the book goes, the bookmark goes. If the book goes to the bottom of the ocean, so does the bookmark. If the book is burned, so is the bookmark. The first chapter of 1 Corinthians establishes the fact that we are "in Christ Jesus." Therefore, like a bookmark, we are in Christ Jesus – and we go wherever He goes!

Later in this same book, 1 Corinthians 15:45, 47, two remarkable names are used of the Lord Jesus: "the last Adam" and "the second man." Scripture does not refer to Him as the second Adam but as "the last Adam;" nor does it refer to Him as the last Man, but as "the second man." The distinction is to be noted, for it enshrines a truth of great value.

As the last Adam, Christ is the sum total of humanity; as the second Man, He is the Head of a new race. So we have here two unions, the one relating to His death and the other to His resurrection. In the first place His union with the race as "the last Adam" began historically at Bethlehem and ended at the Cross and the tomb. In it He gathered up into Himself all that was in Adam and took it to judgment and death on the Cross. In the second place, our union with Him as "the second man" begins in resurrection and ends in eternity – that is, it never ends – for, having in His death done away with the first man in whom God's purpose was frustrated, He rose again as Head of a new race of men, in whom that purpose will at length be fully realized.

When, therefore, the Lord Jesus was crucified on the Cross, He was crucified as the last Adam. All that was in the first Adam was gathered up and done away with in Him. We were included there. As the last Adam, He wiped out the old race. It is in His resurrection that He stands forth as the "second Man," and there, too, we are included. *"For if we have become united with Him by the likeness of His death, we shall be also by the likeness of His resurrection."* (Romans 6:5) We died in Him as the last Adam; we live in Him as the second Man. The Cross is thus the mighty act of God which translated us from Adam to Christ – who bridged the gap and made a way for sinners to become the Sons of God!

God's goal is twofold: First, it is for all things to manifest Christ. In other words, it is for Christ to be Head over all things. Second, it is for man to become like Christ, to have His life and His glory. Today, many believers on earth are lacking in Christ, and many unregenerate souls are manifesting Satan. But God will eventually achieve His goal. One day, all things will manifest Christ. Let us pray that we will be filled with Christ and manifest Him more as befits Sons of God so that God's will can soon be fulfilled!

Chapter Seven
MAN'S DOWNFALL – SIN

As previously mentioned, God's eternal plan is for Christ to be glorified and to be made the Head over all things. But we find in Genesis 3 that when man failed, sin came into the world, and the earth came under the power of Satan. It appeared that all was now lost, and Satan had achieved victory by defeating God and thwarting His plan. However, God foreknew how Satan would rebel and cause all things to be in discord with Him. He also foreknew how man would sin and fall. God therefore held council and Jesus agreed that He would be the "Lamb slain before the foundation of the world!" (Revelation 13:8) It was decided that Jesus would come to earth and become a man who would die on a Cross in order to reconcile all things back to Himself, redeem fallen mankind, and resolve the rebellion of Satan!

Obviously, then, if God the Son must *die* because of it, the matter of sin is exceedingly great! It is fundamental; therefore, the Bible pays a great deal of attention to it. If we want to understand the importance of the salvation provided by God, we must understand what sin is.

According to the Bible, sin is the godless nature within us that motivates us to commit evil *acts* known as *sins*. These are the particular individual acts that we commit outwardly. *Sins* relate to our conduct, while *sin* itself is passed down to us by Adam. Sins are individual acts that are committed by our members: the hands, the feet, the heart, and even the whole body. Paul addresses them when he refers to the practices of the body.

"...You have no obligation whatsoever to do what your sinful nature urges you to do. For if you keep on following it, you will perish. But if through the power of the Holy Spirit you turn from it and its evil deeds, you will live." (Romans 8:12-13)

Sin is referred to by some as "original sin," which drives us toward lust and passion. The Apostle Paul says, *"But sin took advantage of this law and aroused all kinds of forbidden desires within me! ... I know perfectly well that what I am doing is wrong, and my bad conscience shows that I agree that the law is good. But I can't help myself, because it is sin inside me that makes me do these evil things."* (Romans 7:8, 16-17 NLT)

As we have already established, sin is an inner law that controls our members. *"But I see another law in my members, warring against the law of my mind, and bringing me into captivity to the law of sin which is in my members."* (Romans 7:23) It is that force within that compels us to commit evil, and from this we need to be freed. As soon as we are no longer under its power and have nothing to do with it, we will be at peace, able to keep from sinning.

As Romans 6:2 says, *"How shall we, that are dead to sin, live any longer therein?"* and Verses 6-7, *"Knowing this, that our old man is crucified with him, that the body of sin might be destroyed, that henceforth we should not serve sin, for he that is dead, is freed from sin."*

Could we use this illustration, perhaps, to more clearly understand this principle? Imagine that you have a dog. He's a good dog! He never bites, or barks, or has accidents in the house. In fact, he never even runs off! He wants to please his owner who loves him.

However, once in a while a cat might invade his territory. His dog nature overcomes him, and that cat is history! Or, again, let's say that he's chomping on a new bone and the neighbor's dog sneaks over and tries to relieve him of the bone. What dog would lie there and do nothing? No, that good dog is still a dog. He nails that sneak and send him packing.

Now, does the owner go out and shoot his dog for being bad? No. He loves the dog and knows that he will have relapses, and so he forgives his "dog nature."

Of course, we know that a human being and a dog are not in the same category, and no dog can become a human. No owner can pour his spirit into his dog, and transform him. On the other hand, humans can become "little Christs" (or Christians) by the power of the Holy Spirit – with a "new Godly nature," made free from sin, capable of obedience to God.

So the solution to sin, as you can see, comes when we are no longer under its power. In Romans 6, Verse 18, we see this: *"Being then __made free from sin__, you became the servants of righteousness."* And in Verses 22-23, *"But now having __been made__ __free from sin__, __you have your fruit unto__ __holiness__...."* And it follows on to say that it is a gift of God. So, from the sin within, we must be "freed."

The Bible never speaks about being "freed from sins," but always "freed from sin." __*Sins*__, on the other hand, are outside of us, committed one by one, and the only remedy is to be forgiven. Note that the Bible never says "forgiveness of sin" but "forgiveness of sins."

In the entire New Testament, only Romans 5:19 tells who a sinner is: *"For as by one man's disobedience many were made sinners, so by the obedience of one shall many be made righteous."*

So that means everybody! Because we are sinners by birth, we are always sinners, whether we sin or not. A man does not become a sinner because he sins; rather, he sins because he is already a sinner. Remember God's Word: *we __are__ sinners; we do not __become__ sinners*. We have been sinners for a long time already!

For example, let's say you meet someone on the street. You get to talking and at some point you look him right in the eye and say, "You're a sinner!"

Suppose he says, "I can't be a sinner because I've never murdered anyone or missed church on Sunday!"

You reply, "Oh, yes, you are! You're a sinner who has never murdered anyone or missed church on Sunday!"

Suppose someone tells you, "I've never robbed or lied, so I'm not a sinner!"

You reply, "Oh, yes you are! You're a sinner who never robbed or lied."

No matter whom you meet, you can call him a sinner and you'll be right because we are all sinners! (However, I wouldn't recommend this!)

In the beginning mankind lived in Paradise, but was driven out due to disobedience when tempted by Satan. Mankind, through Adam and Eve, failed to trust in God's Word to them. Throughout history, we see that it has been impossible for man – in spite of all his human efforts – to love and obey God enough to keep from sinning. After Adam and Eve fell into sin, they not only failed to regain the earth, but were even taken captive by Satan! Not only was Adam unable to rule, he fell under the rule and power of Satan! Moreover, man even became Satan's *food*, for Genesis 2 tells us that man was made of dust – and Genesis 3 tells us that dust was to be Satan's food! Had you ever thought of that?

The consequence of all this, then, was that man had no way to deal with Satan. Here again, it appeared as though man was doomed. What could be done about this? Did it truly mean that God's eternal purpose for man had failed, and that God's will could not come to pass? Since it is God's desire to have "man" accomplish His purpose and not He Himself, what God could not obtain in the first man (Adam), He achieved in the second man (Jesus). Due to God's determined will and purpose for man to rule, regain the earth, and destroy Satan, this second man (Jesus) was born.

Make no mistake! God *will* have a man to defeat His enemy, Satan. So the Lord Jesus now comes forth, born in a manger in Bethlehem.

Chapter Eight
CHRIST THE SAVIOR IS BORN

The Lord Jesus is the Christ (the Anointed One) of God, as well as the Son of God. This is proclaimed throughout the New Testament and foretold in the Old Testament. (Isaiah 7:14) At the time of His conception, the angel Gabriel told Mary that the child to be born would be the Son of God (Luke 1:35), whereas at the hour of birth, an angel of the Lord announced to the shepherds that the child newly born is Christ the Lord! (Luke 2:11)

At Jesus' baptism, God declared Him to be the Son of God. (Matthew 3:17) Peter acknowledged Jesus as **both** Christ and the Son of God. (Matthew 16:16) On the Mount of Transfiguration, once again God declares Jesus to be His Son. (Matthew 17:5) Romans 1:4 tells us that by His resurrection from the dead, Jesus Christ, our Lord, is declared to be the Son of God. Likewise, Acts 2:36 says He has been made both Lord and Christ by God. As for us, all we need to do is "believe the Scriptures." In believing Jesus as the Christ and as the Son of God we may have life in His name. (John 20:31) *"He who believes in the Son has everlasting life; and he who does not believe in the Son shall not see life, but the wrath of God abides on him."* (John 3:36)

Jesus is Savior because He is Emmanuel, which means "God with us." We read in Matthew that an angel of the Lord appeared to Joseph in a dream and told him, *"Joseph, son of David, do not be afraid to take Mary your wife, for that which is conceived of her is of the Holy Spirit. And she will bring forth a Son, and you shall call His name JESUS, for He will save His people from their sins. So all this was done that it might be fulfilled which was spoken by the Lord through the prophet, saying: 'Behold, the virgin shall be with child, and bear a Son, and they shall call His name Emmanuel, which is translated, 'God with us.'"* (Matthew 1:20-23)

Jesus is Emmanuel; therefore, God and man are both in Jesus. There can be no salvation without Emmanuel. Otherwise, how can unholy man ever touch a holy God? In the Lord Jesus, man and God are at last joined in one. The point of union – or bridge – between God and man is Jesus. In Christ, God and man are reconciled. God is not Emmanuel to us if we are without Christ, since God is not "with us." But in Christ, He is Emmanuel. In Christ, both God and man are "with us."

Jesus is the Son of God from eternity to eternity. He becomes Christ as far back as when the plan of God was laid, before the foundation of the world. As we noted in Chapter One, the Father and the Son held a council. The result was that the Son was to come to the world as a man for the sake of accomplishing the work of redemption – that is, rescuing or literally ransoming mankind from eternal death.

Listen to the Word from Ephesians 1:4:

"According as he hath chosen us in him before the foundation of the world, that we should be holy and without blame before him in love; having predestined us unto the adoption of children by Jesus Christ to himself, according to the good pleasure of his will."

Therefore, the coming of Christ to this world was not an emergency act; it came out of the foreordained plan of God. This was necessary because man had "infected" himself with sin, and sin, by definition, is "separation from God."

God created us so as to satisfy the heart of Christ, and His redemptive plan was to reconcile all things to Himself. But the first step in the redemptive plan of Christ was the necessity of His birth. In becoming a man (the incarnation) He stepped down from the position of the Creator to the place of the created. By taking upon Himself the body of the created, He was able to die for man and for all creation. Since "all things" were created in Christ (Colossians 1:16, and John 1:3), God was able to deal with them when He accepted Jesus' sacrificial death on our behalf. In Christ, therefore, everything has been reconciled by God. This accomplishes His first purpose: that all things might manifest the glory of the Lord Jesus Christ.

Chapter Nine
REDEMPTION OF FALLEN MANKIND

God creates to accomplish His plan. He created all things and man with the intent that all things might manifest Christ, especially man – who would be like Christ, having His life and glory. But Satan rebelled and interfered, with the result that man fell into sin. In the fullness of time, God countered his move by *redemption* in order to regain the purpose of His creation. Christ's all-inclusive death on the Cross reconciled all things to God and, by the power of the Holy Spirit, His resurrection redeemed fallen mankind by imparting His life to man.

The redemption of Christ imparted His life to man, accomplishing God's second purpose. In the work of redemption, Christ not only reconciled all things to God, but also gave life to man so that man might be like Him. This is the release of the Holy Spirit into man's spirit. Christ has the preeminence in redemption: He solved the rebellion of Satan, and resolved the sin of man.

The aim of redemption is to let Christ have the pre-eminence in all things. The redemption of Christ realized God's plan which was laid before the foundation of the world. (Genesis 1:26-27; Romans 5:14) This was done so that Christ might have first place in all things.

But redemption does not alter God's purpose; instead it fulfills that purpose which creation had earlier failed to do. God had originally designed man to have dominion and to rule over the earth, but alas, as we've said, man fell. Nevertheless, not everything was finished and done for because the first man had fallen. As stated before, what God could not obtain in the first man (Adam), He achieved in the second Man (Christ). Due to God's determined will and purpose for man to rule, regain the earth, and destroy Satan as one created (man) against another created (Satan), there occurred the birth of Jesus in Bethlehem. God will have a man to defeat His enemy. So the Lord Jesus now comes forth, to save man from being the food – which is the "dust" Satan must eat as seen in Genesis 3:14 – to recover the earth; and to save man from his sins.

For example, some years ago, as a Christian, I realized that God had blessed me and my family greatly. However, just when I thought I had everything under control, it seemed that one adversity after another pulled me down. It took awhile, but then I began to realize that God was using these trials as the "chastisement of the Lord" to bring me to the point where I understood that I valued "the good life" more than Him.

At that point, overcome with regret, I realized anew the amazing love that Christ had for me, and decided to forsake lesser things and consecrate myself to God, so that His original purpose in creating me might be achieved. I began to understand that God's plan, in addition to spreading the Gospel message, was for the Church – me included as a joint heir with Christ – to drive out Satan from this earth and rule here for Him.

Let me note here that, according to our laws, when a man dies and leaves his last will and testament to his children, once the will is probated, the children are entitled to appropriate their inheritance. Just so, they didn't have to *die* to inherit his riches. The *man* had to die. Then it became the children's property. From this you can see that *Jesus died* and left His saints His inheritance to use now – because He has already died! Isn't that awesome? We can use His Name to drive the devil out of our Garden and bring Him glory on earth, *now!* We don't have to die to get that power – it wouldn't do us any good in Heaven! We need to use it now! Friends, let this truth sink into your hearts and begin to use the Word and please the Father as we pull down the devil's strongholds by faith. (2 Corinthians 10:4-5)

It's become my passion that my mission in the Church is to testify to the salvation of Christ on the one hand, and to the victory of Christ over Satan on the other. I'm convinced that God is pleased when His children see their role as part of the Church, as they go out conquering our Adversary.

We must always view redemption as an interruption, an emergency measure, made necessary by a catastrophic break in the straight line of the purpose of God. Redemption is big enough and wonderful enough, to occupy a very large place in our vision, but God is saying that we should not make redemption to be everything, as though man was created to be redeemed. The Fall was indeed a tragic dip downward in that line of "purpose," and the atonement a blessed recovery whereby our sins are blotted out and we are reunited with God (restored). Yet, when this was accomplished, there yet remained a work to be done to bring us into possession of that which Adam never possessed – and to give God what His heart most desired. You see, God has never forsaken the purpose which is represented by the straight line. Adam was never in possession of the life of God as presented in the "tree of life." But because of the one work of the Lord Jesus in His death and resurrection (and it must be emphasized that it is all one work!), His life was released to become ours by faith, and *we have received more than Adam ever possessed!*

Now, the very purpose of God is brought within reach of fulfillment in us by our "receiving Christ as our life," or, in other words, by our regeneration. The whole plan of redemption was to exalt and glorify man, because God's preordained plan and election was to obtain a glorious man – one who can and will exercise dominion over the earth.

The only condition for God's salvation is faith. This faith is to believe in the Word of God. What is the Word of God? Here are a few Scriptures to remember:

"And the Word became flesh and dwelt among us, and we beheld His glory, the glory as of the only begotten of the Father, full of grace and truth." (John 1:14)

"I am the way, the truth, and the life. No one can come to the Father except through Me." (John 14:6)

"For by grace you have been saved through faith, and that not of yourselves; it is the gift of God, not of works, lest anyone should boast." (Ephesians 2:8-9)

"Anyone who believes and is baptized will be saved. But anyone who refuses to believe will be condemned." (Matthew 28:16)

"I assure you, anyone who believes in Me already has eternal life." (John 6:47)

"He who has the Son has the life; he who does not have the Son of God does not have the life. I have written these things to you that you may know that you have eternal life, to you who believe into the name of the Son of God." (1 John 5:12-13)

"I am the resurrection and the life; he who believes in me, even if he should die, shall live." (John 11:25)

"Therefore I said to you that you will die in your sins; for unless you believe that "I Am," you will die in you sins." (John 8:24)

"The blood of Jesus His Son cleanses us from every sin." (1John 1:7)

"And as Moses lifted up the serpent in the wilderness, even so must the Son of Man be lifted up, that who ever believes in Him should not perish, but have eternal life." (John 3:14-15)

"For God so loved the world that He gave His only begotten Son, that everyone who believes on Him may not perish, but have eternal life." (John 3:16)

46

"He who believes in the Son has everlasting life; and he who does not believe in the Son shall not see life, but the wrath of God that abides on him." (John 3:36)

"There is therefore no condemnation to those who are in Christ Jesus." (Romans 8:1)

"Therefore whoever confesses Me before men, him I will also confess before My Father who is in heaven." (Matthew 10:32)

Redemption is the "Divine" way of deliverance. We were born sinners; how then can we cut off our sinful heredity? Seeing that we were born in Adam, how can we get out of Adam? There is only one way: since we came in by birth we must go out by death. To do away with our sinfulness we must do away with our life. Slavery to sin came by birth; deliverance from sin comes by death – and it is just this way of escape that God has provided. *"We died ... to sin."* (Romans 6:2)

God created man in order for man to be like Christ, having the life as well as His glory. As God manifests Himself through Christ, so He manifests Himself through man. We are called by God in order that we might become partakers of His Son, made to be conformed to His image so that His Son might become the Firstborn among many brethren. From eternity past up to the resurrection, the Lord was "the only begotten Son." But after He was raised from the dead, He became the Firstborn Son.

Accordingly, after the resurrection He said to Mary Magdalene: *"Go unto my brethren, and say to them, I ascend unto my Father and your Father."* (Emphasis mine) (John 20:17) While Jesus was on earth He could not say to His disciples *"...and your Father."* God the Father accepted them as "sons" only after Christ's work of redemption was completed. These many sons became sons "in" the only begotten Son. By the death of God's only begotten Son, many sons were born.

The grain of wheat mentioned in John 12:24 is symbolic of God's only begotten Son. The life of the wheat was hidden inside the husk. If the seed (Jesus Christ, the Son of God) had not fallen into the ground and died, it would have been alone. But if it died, the husk would decompose and the inner life would be liberated so as to bear many grains (many sons). Each one of the many grains would resemble the first grain. Yet, it can also be said that each one of the grains is in that one grain.

Christ died to beget (become the father of) us. Before death, He was the only begotten Son. After resurrection He became the firstborn Son among many sons. By the resurrection of Christ, God begets us and gives us His life. Hence, the death of Christ was the great emancipation of the life of Christ! Through His death, He distributed His life to us, thereby accomplishing God's second purpose. As noted before, all that is left for us to do is "believe." Faith in the accomplished works of Christ is all that remains in order for every one of us to obtain everlasting (eternal) life.

"For God so loved the world, that He gave His only begotten Son, that every one who believes on Him may not perish, but have eternal life." (John 3:16)

48

Chapter Ten
PAUL'S PRAYER FOR
WISDOM AND REVELATION

As we begin to know God, His work, and His eternal plan which He purposed in eternity past, we begin to realize that the apostle Paul's "revelation" in Ephesians is beyond special! Through the Holy Spirit, he was led to pray two prayers recorded in this Book. One prayer is found in Chapter One, and it is basic, while the other is found in Chapter Three and is for the building. In Chapter One, Paul prayed that we would realize our relationship with the Lord. In Chapter Three, he wanted us not only to realize our relationship with the Lord, but also our relationship with the Church.

In Ephesians 1:17, Paul prayed, *"That the God of our Lord Jesus Christ, the Father of glory, may give to you a spirit of wisdom and revelation in the full knowledge of Him."* Why did Paul want the believers to have a spirit of wisdom and revelation? He knew they were going to need these gifts in order for them to know the following three things:

(1) *"The full knowledge of Him."* (Verse 17) This means to know God Himself.

(2) *"The hope of His calling, and what are the riches of the glory of His inheritance in the saints"* (Verse 18) This refers to God's eternal plan and its final accomplishment. God's "calling" is for us to be His sons. These sons are His inheritance. We have established that God's calling was made before the foundation of the

world. In the coming eternity, He will have an inheritance in the saints, an inheritance that is full of the riches of glory! In eternity past, God made a decision, and in eternity future God will reap a reward. These two things added together make up God's eternal plan and its goal. Paul was trying to make known to us the eternal plan of God.

(3) *"The surpassing greatness of His power toward us who believe."* (Verse 19) This refers to the kind of power God uses today to reach His goal and accomplish His plan. We need to receive revelation from the Lord in order to understand these few things.

Early on, after we first receive the gift of faith from God and believe in His Son, Jesus Christ, we think we know quite a bit about God! Yet we often depend a great deal on *our* knowledge (not Divine wisdom), and our feelings, (not inner faith), to support us on our lifelong journey. Without wisdom and faith to support us, our knowledge of God is sketchy and our understanding is unsound. Therefore, we often need the support of our mind in maintaining our Christian walk. If we encounter obstacles in our reasoning or in our doctrines, we find that we cannot go on without the help of our mind. At other difficult times we need feelings, feelings of joy, and feelings of exuberance just to get by.

At last, God gives to us a spirit of wisdom and revelation. Then He reveals Himself to us in a fresh, special, and deepening way, so that we can say that not only do we "know" Him, but we have a full knowledge of Him. Then we can say, "Now I know. I have seen, and I am clear. I do not need any other help. I do not need my mind or my feelings to support me anymore. I have the full knowledge of God now." In other words, "revelation" enables us to see what God sees. (Hebrews 4:13)

This is indeed a crucial matter. Many Christians live by their feelings. If they feel happy and joyful, they say that God has been gracious to them. If they feel cold and indifferent, and if they lose their zest for life, they often say, "Where is God?" Many people are sustained by their feelings. Once their feelings are gone, they become shaky and unsure of themselves. Why? Because they do not have the full knowledge of God. In Proverbs 1:7, 33, Solomon tells us, *"The fear of the Lord is the beginning of knowledge, but fools despise wisdom and instruction ... whoever listens to me will dwell safely, and will be secure, without fear of evil."*

God has to lead us to the point where we no longer care if we feel happy or sad, indifferent or excited, because we have known God. Our knowledge is deeper than our happiness, our pain, or our feelings. Although outwardly there may be happiness, pain, or feelings of excitement or sadness, none of this will change our inner peace because we know Him inwardly. This is the kind of Christian we should all strive to become, because this kind will stand, not be shaken, and is a *"...vessel meet for the Master's use."* (2 Timothy 2:21)

Revelation is indispensable. *"Where there is no revelation, the people cast off restraint; but happy is he who keeps the law."* (Proverbs 28:18) We need to ask God to give us a spirit of revelation, so that we can have the full knowledge of Him. This knowledge is foundational to a believer. Paul's main point to his prayer for the saints in Ephesians, Chapter 1, was that they would receive a spirit of wisdom and revelation so that their eyes would be opened to see some valuable truths.

The one thing Ephesians, Chapter 1 speaks of is that all of God's works are finished. We don't need God to do more works, but we need to have the revelation concerning the works that He has already completed. God has planned and purposed. Today, God's children need to know His plan and His purpose. *"He who comes forward to God must believe that He is."* (Hebrews 11:6) God is He who is; He never changes.

Today, we need revelation to see God. The apostle prayed that God would grant us a spirit of wisdom and revelation in the full knowledge of Him who already "is," that we would have a full knowledge of His predetermined plan, and understand His accomplished works. Many people hope that God will add some new arrangements and implement some new works in His plan.

In his book, "The Prayer Ministry of the Church," Watchman Nee says, "God has many things stacked up in Heaven. He cannot accomplish any of them because there is no outlet for him on earth. Brothers and sisters, you have to remember that the highest and greatest work of the Church is to be the outlet of God's will through prayer."

He also says, "In Heaven, God's power is unlimited. But on earth, God's power is manifested to the degree that the Church prays. The Church must have big prayers to manifest our God. This is the ministry of the Church. It is not a question of how often we pray. It is a question of the weight of our prayer. If we see the Church's responsibility of prayer, we will see that our prayers are not big enough; we are limiting God and frustrating His work. The Church has forsaken its duty! What a sad situation this is!"

It's not a matter of wishing God's plan would be this or that; God has arranged everything already, and we only need to see what He has set in order – and travail in prayer until it comes to pass on earth! Remember James told us that *"...the effectual <u>fervent</u> prayer of a righteous man availeth much."* (James 5:15)

God doesn't need to do one more thing; He's only waiting for us to see what He's *already* done. Once we see, we will have a fresh experience. We need a "spirit of wisdom" to understand His work, and we need a "spirit of revelation" to know what He has done. Only then will we become useful people in God's eyes.

Chapter Eleven
THE CHURCH

So, what is "the Church?" We get our word "church" from the Greek word "ekklesia." "Ek" means "to come out" while "klesia" means "to congregate or to gather." Thus, *ekklesia* means the gathering of those who have been "called out of the world." According to Scripture, the Church is both "the Body and the Bride of Christ." (Revelation 19:7 NAS)

So, the Church is made up of those who have been redeemed by the blood, who have been regenerated by the Holy Spirit, who have committed themselves into God's hands, and who are willing to take God's will – and *do* it! This body of believers stands for God on earth for the sake of maintaining His testimony.

As such, what position is the Church to maintain on earth today? Why does God permit Satan, whose head is already crushed, to remain on earth? I believe that He permits Satan to remain for the sake of creating opportunities for Her to win victories for His Son. Christ, the Head, has ascended, but His Body is still on earth! The Church, as His Body, is His propagation, left here to wage warfare against God's enemy, the devil.

She is not only to preach the Gospel to save sinners, but using the gifts He gave Her, demonstrate the victory of Christ on the Cross. Her responsibility is to continue the warfare that He fought on earth. However, the Church today is malnourished and weak, unable to perform her task. And why?

As a doctor, I see a lot of ailments of the physical, human body, caused in large part by our own faults. We get careless or take foolish chances and end up injuring ourselves. We put substances into our bodies that we know cause them harm and good medical advice is often ignored.

For instance, many people consume alcohol socially to keep up with the crowd. They get into their cars, take off, and think they're in control. Then a tragedy occurs. They miss a stop sign or traffic light – and injure or kill someone else. Doctors like myself often see these individuals brought into the ER by ambulance – bloody, unconscious, on the verge of death all because of their (or someone else's) care-less attitude.

But why? The answer is because we are self-grati-fying by nature, and we despise any kind of accountability!

This all stems from our complicity with Satan in the Garden of Eden: why should we obey God and abstain from eating of the Tree of Knowledge of Good and Evil? Satan deceived Eve by saying that God forbade them because if they did eat of it, 1), they would not surely die, and, 2), they would become as He is, all-powerful and all-knowing. If man had just listened to God and eaten of the Tree of Life – in essence obeying Christ – everything that he really needed would have been provided for him in accordance with God's Word. Hence, this freedom of choice issue got us into trouble from the beginning of time, and still haunts us today. Many of us have not yet understood that there is no real freedom without accountability and responsibility.

There is a most marvelous correlation between the fleshly body of man and the spiritual Body of Christ, which is the Church. Our conscience (in essence, "head") tells us one thing but our self-will ("body") does otherwise. We hear from the doctor that good health habits, put into action, will bring about a strong, healthy, body, and our minds agree. We all pretty much know what these are, but we ignore his advice. Sooner, rather that later, weakness and disease will set in.

This same scenario can be seen in the Church today. When there is spiritual discord between the Body's desires and the guidance of Christ (the Head), strife follows. Prayer, fellowship, and love for one another are the spiritual necessities (good habits) of the Body, the Church. These virtues are seriously lacking in believers and the Church today. Without these fervent practices exercised continuously by all Christians, the will of God cannot and will not be carried out on earth.

We all want to be strong and healthy, physically, and know it requires work and diligence for that to be accomplished. Likewise, for the Church to be strong and healthy on earth today, our Omnipotent "Doctor" (God) demands that certain exercises be carried out before His promises can be fulfilled. It is all up to us; God despises slothfulness! (Matthew 25:26)

Listening to authority is something mankind is getting worse at doing today more than ever before in history! God gave us His Holy Spirit to be our spiritual guide and authority after Jesus ascended to Heaven, but He is largely overlooked by many Christians. We prefer to seek our own paths. Jesus, Himself, said in John 5:19 (NIV), *"I tell you the truth, the Son can do nothing by Himself; He can do only what He sees the Father doing because whatever the Father does the Son also does."* And in John 6:38, He states: *"For I have come down from heaven not to do my will but to do the will of him that has sent me."* If Jesus' life was so directed by God the Father, how can we live our lives by anything less? After all, if it is true that our quality of life would be much better if we would only listen to our doctor, just imagine how much more spiritually blessed we would be if we communicated in prayer and listened and obeyed "His" guidance in all our thoughts, words, and actions!

After all, Jesus said, *"Abide in Me, and I in you. As the branch cannot bear fruit of itself, unless it abides in the vine, neither can you, unless you abide in Me. I am the vine, you are the branches. He who abides in Me, and I in him, bears much fruit; for without Me you can do nothing."* (John 15:4-5)

For this reason, the Church must be that which is "taken out" of Christ (where we abide). This union was foreseen in the Garden of Eden when Eve was "taken out" of Adam.

When God began the human race, he made Adam out of the dust of the earth. Adam became flesh and blood, living in the form of a man. Note, however, Eve was not made from dust! God didn't repeat Himself when He created Woman. Instead, He created Eve from Adam's rib! In other words, she "came out" of Adam. In short, Eve *was* part of Adam.

Can you see how only that which "came out" of Adam could be Adam's helpmeet? Remember that when all the birds of the heavens were brought to Adam, he could not find a helpmeet among them because none of them had come out of him? Similarly, when all the cattle were brought before him, Adam again failed to find his helpmeet among them, because they too had not come of him. Likewise, all the beasts of the field were rejected, for their origin was also wrong. Not one from among all these potential candidates had "come out" of Adam; therefore, not one of them could qualify.

Who, then, *could* be found? Only Eve. She, too, was brought to Adam just as the birds, the cattle, and the beasts had been brought. But there was a basic difference between Eve and these living creatures: Eve alone had qualified. And as a result, she could become Adam's bride! She came out of him, and she returned to him. In short, what came out of Adam was his *body*; what returned to him was his *bride* as stated in Genesis 2:24! *"For this cause a man shall leave his father and his mother, and shall cleave to his wife; and they shall become one flesh."*

There is no doubt from the Scriptures that Adam was created first and Eve created second, with God declaring them as two; but He also declares that these two are to become one flesh! *"The two shall become one flesh."* (Ephesians 5:31b) This all foretells the relationship between the Church and Christ: from one there becomes two, and from two there becomes one. In the beginning when God created man, He created male and female. But Eve "came out of" Adam, so Eve and Adam were one. By the same token, the Church "comes out of" Christ, so She and Christ are one. Yet Eve was "with" Adam, therefore she and Adam were separate entities. Likewise, the Church is "with" Christ, and thus the Church is distinct from Christ. Therefore, we may say that speaking of union, the two are one; but speaking of distinction, the one becomes two.

These two different positions are also shown in relation to time. Today, the Church is the Body of Christ and as such She is to manifest the life of Christ. One day, however, the Book of Revelation tells us that this spiritual Church will be brought by God to Christ to be His *Bride!*

Even as Adam is a type of Christ, the Church is but another form of Him – even as Eve was the other form of Adam.

From this we can see that the Church *is* Christ. Many think that the gathering together of believers makes up "the Church." This concept is far from the truth. The true Church is that part which is "taken out of Christ" and *not* what is naturally made from dust. She is the Bride created by God with Christ as Her source and not the natural man made of dust. Only that which comes out of Christ can go back to Him. What does not come out of Him can never return to Him. But that which comes from Heaven *can* return there. Today, whenever we speak of *home,* we are referring to the place from whence we came. To *return home* is to go back to that place. So, too, is the spiritual realm: if we have not come from Heaven, we will not be able to return there.

A person's fleshly skill, intelligence, ability, power – and everything else that is of man himself – are all outside of the Church. That which comes from Christ alone is in the Church. Eve was created from Adam, a picture – a type – of the Church and Christ. This is a most precious truth! That which came out of Adam (and not that which came from dust) was called Eve. Whatever does not come out of Christ has no relationship to the Church.

God will never use the old creation (fleshly things) to build the new creation (spiritual things). The Lord Jesus tells us: *"...that which is born of the Spirit is spirit, and that which is born of the flesh is flesh."* (John 3:6) He will never use the fleshly to produce the spiritual. The source is what counts. Our works here on earth must originate in the Spirit for God to count them as useful, no matter how good our goal may seem to be. All our talent and ingenuity must first be dealt with by the Cross in order to have spiritual usefulness.

For example, a person could be quite clever, having a high level of intelligence. Formerly, he might have used his brain to research philosophy, science or literature. But, once he is saved, he employs this same clear and able brain in researching the Word of God. The question is: where did this brilliant intellect originate? Has it been dealt with by the Cross? Has it come under the control of the Holy Spirit? If his I.Q. is purely something with which he was born, and not dealt with by the Cross, then it belongs to earthly Adam. It originates out of *self,* the natural – in other words, out of the flesh. Although he may have changed the subject matter – the object of his research now being God's Word – his brain remains the same old entity. An unrenewed mind cannot understand the Bible, nor will it be able to help the Church. On the contrary, it will damage Her.

God must bring down all of our natural virtues before we are prepared to fulfill our destinies. Have you ever noticed how, throughout the Bible, God takes a person and breaks his pride in himself before that one becomes what God intended?

Take Moses, for example. Through God's supernatural outworkings, Moses becomes part of the royal family. He lives in the palace, he has the finest education Egypt could offer, and he walks among men in Pharoah's court as a prince.

Then, in his own strength, thinking God will be pleased that he defends one of his fellow Hebrews from a cruel master, he kills the man. He buries him, thinking no one knows. However, word gets out, and Moses must run for his life into the desert. The only work he can find there is as a shepherd – the lowest of professions! So low, in fact, that a shepherd's testimony in court was not permitted!

For 40 years he lives as an outcast in the land of Midian with his wife and children. It gets so bad that Moses cannot even speak without stuttering! But the day comes when God meets him in a burning bush – and from that day on, everything changes. This time his authority is from God, not Pharoah!

Then – in the power of God – Moses goes back to Egypt, delivers the entire nation of Israel, and brings them to the Promised Land with many miracles to his credit.

The same can be said of Saul of Tarsus. A brilliant man – well-educated, well-to-do, and zealous for God – he thought he was doing Him a favor when he persecuted the young Church. Powerful, vehement, and sure of himself, he learns on the road to Damascus that he is nothing. He is, in fact, persecuting God's Son! It takes many years, but at last the Apostle Paul is elevated to a place of honor in the courts of Heaven and wound up writing most of the New Testament – giving glory to Jesus, God's Son.

Notice from this that there is a time of preparation before we are ready to receive authority and assume our duties. Our natural strengths must be dealt with by the

Cross. We must bow to the control of the Holy Spirit; otherwise we will do damage to the Church.

The Church is not established by adding a few Christians to some other Christians in a certain building. Neither is it a large group of people. The Church shares one life in common – She shares the one Christ. You possess a portion of Christ, another possesses a portion of Him, and everyone possesses a portion. By gathering together the Christ in all these people, the Church comes into being.

Every true Christian knows the life in Christ; yet, sadly, not all Christians know the life in the Body of Christ. As the life of Christ is a reality, so too is the life of the Body. Christians are not to remain fragments, they are to be united into one – even as Paul once wrote, declaring: *"Seeing that we who are many are one bread, one body."* (1 Corinthians 10.17a) If you live by Christ, you will be one with all Christians. We know that, henceforth, we must do all things according to the principle of mutual help, of fellowship, and of the Body through the power of the indwelling Holy Spirit. However, if you live by your own fleshly life, you will be separated from the children of God.

Since the Church is the Body of Christ, you need to know that within the Body there is an inherent law. Every member has his gift, and every member is governed by a strange and mysterious Law of Function. It is imperative for the members to learn how to be subject to the Law of the Body. If any member should act independently, selfishly doing what he wants, it betrays a sickness. The characteristic of the Body is oneness, but when that oneness is broken, the Body is sick.

As a medical doctor, let me draw a parallel here.

One who insists upon acting alone, with no regard to the cautions of other members of the Body, becomes an uncontrollable, malignant cell in the Body. That person will contribute to its destruction. He or she will become a cancer, its cells rapidly multiplying, unable to function with others, totally independent, and detrimental to the Body.

Can you see, therefore, that we must learn to accept the judgment of the Body and learn to flow with its movement of life? For this reason, no child of God should violate the Law of the Body of Christ and act independently. Independent actions always speak of rebellion.   To act independently is to reject the authority of the Head, which God has ordained for the Body. Independent action is a matter both of disobedience to the Lord and insubordination to the Body.

Those who act this way, who reject the control of the Body and follow their own whims, who do not learn to obey the authority of the Head, cause dissension. After we have believed in the Lord, the first spiritual principle we should remember is that the Body is God's ordained authority on earth.

As you become a mature Christian, the more you see that the oneness (interdependence) of the members of the Body must function in harmony. Authority must be distributed upon each cell and each must work together, not independently. This is most marvelous. How appropriate it is that Scripture uses the physical body as an illustration of the Church!

We must quit trying to produce Godly works out of ourselves. This doesn't mean that we aren't zealous to please Him; it simply means that all our zeal must originate with the Lord. It's not that we won't work, but that we will only do what He gives us to do. We need power, but we must seek the power that comes from Him. The entire issue lies in this matter of source: where has it originated? In John 5:19a we read that the Lord Jesus declared: *"The Son can do nothing of himself."* If Jesus can't, then how can we, His followers, ever do anything on our own accord? We must realize that we can do nothing on our own. I repeat that Jesus gave us a clue to this when He said, *"I am the vine, you are the* *branches; he who abides in Me and I in him, he bears much fruit, for <u>apart from Me you can do nothing</u>."* (John 15:5 NASB)

In conclusion, we must remember that the Cross of Christ produced the Church, and the Church is ordained to bring in the Kingdom. Therefore, in these last days before the Lord returns, She stands between the Cross and the Kingdom. The present age is the time for Her to practice the victory of Christ. The Head has overcome; now the Body must also overcome by the power of the Holy Spirit. The Lord destroyed the devil on the Cross, produced the Church, and gave Her resurrection life. Today, God is establishing His Kingdom on earth through His Church. She must continue to *"...heal the sick, raise the dead and cleanse the lepers."* (Matthew 10:8) She must *"...pull down the devil's strongholds."* (2 Corinthians 10:4 KJV) by way of prayer, knowing the will of God, and carry on the victorious work that Christ began against Satan. She has a Heavenly mandate to bring Heaven's will down to earth and occupy until he comes.

Jesus made it clear as recorded in the Four Gospels that we are to "occupy until he returns." (Luke 19:13) Let Him not be grieved as He considers the condition of the Church for whom He died.

Look at the words of an old hymn that says it better than I can:

Rise Up, O Men of God!

Rise up, O men of God!
Have done with lesser things;
Give heart and soul and mind and strength
To serve the King of kings.
Rise up, O men of God! His Kingdom tarries long;
Bring in the day of brotherhood
and end the night of wrong.
Rise up, O men of God!

The Church for you doth wait.
Her strength unequal to her task;
Rise up, and make her great!
Lift high the Cross of Christ!
Tread where His feet have trod;
As brothers of the Son of Man,
Rise up, O men of God!
(by William P. Merrill and William H. Walter)
(Great Hymns of the Faith, Singspiration Music, 1974)

Chapter Twelve
THE REVELATION OF
THE BLOOD OF CHRIST

Let us begin with the precious Blood of the Lord Jesus Christ and its value to us in dealing with our sins and justifying us in the sight of God. As we know, when sin came into the world it found expression in an act of disobedience to God. *"For as by one man's disobedience many were made sinners, so also by one Man's obedience many will be made righteous."* (Romans 5:19) To redeem us and bring us back to the purpose of God, the Lord Jesus had to do something about all the consequences of sin.

The first problem was, *"They are all under sin."* (Romans 3:9)

Secondly, man's awakened conscience said, *"I have sinned."* (Luke 15:18) That sin in man, which from then on constituted a barrier to man's fellowship with God, gave rise to a sense of *guilt* in man and estrangement from God. Sin also provided Satan with his ground of accusation before God, while our sense of guilt gave him his ground of accusation in our hearts.

Lastly, it is *"the accuser of the brethren"* (Revelation 12:10) who now says, "You have sinned."

To redeem us, therefore, and to bring us back to the purpose of God, the Lord Jesus had to do something about these three questions of sin, guilt, and Satan's charge against us. Our sins had first to be dealt with, and this was effected by the precious Blood of Christ. Our guilt has to be dealt with and our guilty conscience relieved by showing us the value of that Blood. And finally, the attack of the enemy has to be confronted and his accusations refuted. In the Scriptures, the Blood of Christ is shown to have operated effectually in these three ways: toward God, toward man, and toward Satan.

In the first eight chapters of Romans, two aspects of salvation are presented to us: first, the forgiveness of our sins, and second, our deliverance from sin. Here, also, is reference to the Blood of the Lord Jesus, in Chapter 3:25 *"Whom God has set forth to be a propitiation through faith in his blood, to declare his righteousness for the remission of sins that are past, through the forbearance of God...."* and in Chapter 5:9, *"Much more then, being now justified by his blood, we shall be saved from wrath through him."*

This part centers around that aspect of the Lord Jesus which is represented by "the Blood" shed for our justification through "the remission of sins." This tells us the Blood deals with what we have done and disposes of our sins. It is a question of sins (plural) that we have committed before God. Later on, we will discuss the second section of Romans 1-8, and see the work of "the Cross" and how it deals with what we are, and the one sin-principle in each of us that leads us to repeatedly sin, and how it delivers us from the power of sin (singular).

The Blood is for atonement (Jesus' sacrificial death paid the penalty for our sins) and has to do first with our standing before God. We need forgiveness for the sins we have committed, or we will come under judgment; and they are forgiven, not because God overlooks what we have done, but because He sees the Blood. The Blood is therefore not primarily for us, but for God! If I want to understand the value of the Blood, I must accept God's valuation, and if I do not know something of the value set upon the Blood by God I shall never know what its value is for me. Indeed, it is only as the estimate that God puts upon the Blood of Christ is made known to me by His Holy Spirit that I find how precious the Blood is to me. But the first aspect of it is toward God. Throughout the Old and New Testaments the word "blood" is used in connection with the idea of atonement, and throughout it is something for God.

One example of this is described in Exodus 12:13, where there is the shedding of the blood of the Passover lamb in Egypt for Israel's redemption from the death of the firstborn. This is one of the best examples in the Old Testament of our redemption. The blood was put outside on the lintel and door-posts, whereas the meat, the flesh of the lamb, was eaten inside the house; and God said: *"When I see the blood, I will pass over you."*

Here is another illustration of the fact that the blood was not meant to be presented to man, but to God, for the blood was put on the lintel and on the door-posts, where those feasting inside the house would not see it. The blood is solely for God's satisfaction.

It is God's holiness, God's righteousness, which demands that a sinless life should be given for man. There is life in the Blood, and that Blood has to be poured out (shed) for me, for my sins. God is the One who requires it to be so. God is the One who demands that the Blood be presented, in order to satisfy His own righteousness, and it is He who says: *"When I see the blood, I will pass over you."* The Blood of Christ fully satisfies God.

The Blood is first for God to see. We then have to accept God's valuation of it. In doing so we shall find our salvation. If, instead, we try to come to a valuation by way of our feelings, we get nothing; we remain in darkness. No, it is a matter of faith in God's Word. We have to believe that the Blood is precious to God because He says it is so. (1 Peter 1:18-19) If God can accept the Blood as a payment for our sins and as the price of our redemption, then we can rest assured that the debt has been paid! If God is satisfied with the Blood, then the Blood must be acceptable. Our valuation of it is only according to His valuation – no more, no less. It cannot, or course, be more, but it must not be less. Always remember that He is holy and He is righteous, and that a holy and righteous God has the right to say that the Blood is acceptable in His eyes and has fully satisfied Him.

Therefore, if the Blood has satisfied God; it must satisfy us also. This is the second value of the Blood, that is, toward man, in the cleansing of our conscience. Hebrews 10:22, says that the Blood does this, that we are to have *"...hearts sprinkled from an evil conscience."* It does not tell us that the Blood of the Lord Jesus cleanses our hearts, and then stops there. It is not enough to assume that this means it is proper to pray, "Lord, cleanse my heart from sin by thy Blood." The heart, God says, is *"desperately sick"* (Jeremiah 17:9) and He must do something more fundamental than merely cleanse it: He must give us a new one. *"A new heart also will I give you, and a new Spirit will I put within you."* (Ezekiel 36:26) The work of the Blood is wholly objective before God. This does not say that the Blood cleanses our hearts. True, the cleansing work of the Blood is seen here in Hebrews10 to have reference to the heart, but it is in relation to the conscience. But what does this mean?

It means that there was something intervening between myself and God, as a result of which I had an evil conscience whenever I sought to approach Him. It was constantly reminding me of the barrier that stood between myself and Him. But now, through the operation of the precious Blood of Christ, something new has been effected before God which has removed that barrier, and God has made that fact known to me in His Word. When that has been believed and accepted, my conscience is at once cleared and my sense of guilt removed, and I have no more an evil conscience toward God.

Every one of us knows what a precious thing it is to have a clear conscience, void of offense, in our dealings with God. A heart of faith and a conscience clear of any and every accusation are both equally essential to us, since they are interdependent. As soon as we find our conscience is uneasy, our faith leaks away, and immediately we know we cannot face God. In order, therefore, to keep going on with God, we must know the up-to-date value of the Blood. God keeps short accounts, and we come closer to God by the Blood of His Son every day, every hour and every minute. It never loses it efficacy as our ground of access if we will but lay hold upon it. When we enter the Most Holy Place, on what ground dare we enter but by the Blood?

What do I mean when I say, "by the Blood"? I simply mean that I recognize my sins, that I confess that I have need of cleansing and of atonement, and that I come to God on the basis of the finished work of the Lord Jesus. I approach God through His merit alone, and never on the basis of my attainment: never, for example, on the ground that I attended mass every Sunday for the past year, or that I did something good for the Lord this morning. I have to come by way of the Blood every time. A clear conscience in order to approach God is never based upon our attainment; it can only be based on the work of the Lord Jesus in the shedding of His Blood.

Some of us are unsure of the proper way to approach God. Some think in terms such as these: "Today I've been doing a little better; this morning I felt uplifted when I read the Bible, so today I can pray better!" Or again, "Today I was in strife with the family; my day started out cloudy and depressing, so I'd better not approach God."

What, after all, is your basis of approach to God? Do you come to Him on the shaky ground of your feelings? Do you depend upon the feeling that you may have achieved something for God today? Or is your approach based on something far more secure, namely, the fact that the Blood has been shed, and that God looks on the Blood and is satisfied? Of course, were it conceivably possible for the Blood to suffer any change, the basis for your approach to

God might be less trustworthy. But the Blood has never changed and never will.

Your approach to God is therefore always in **boldness**; and that boldness is yours through the Blood and never through your personal good deeds. Whatever you count as your "holy merits" today or yesterday or the day before, as soon as you make a conscious move into the Most Holy Place (wherever you meet and commune with God one on One), immediately you have to take your stand upon the safe and only ground of the Blood of His Son. Whether you have had a good day or a bad day, your basis of approach is always the same – the Blood of Christ. God's acceptance of that Blood is the ground upon which you may enter, and there is no other.

This does not mean that we should not pray or live a careless life, for the next part of our discussion on the death of Christ will show us that anything but is contemplated. But for now let us be satisfied with the Blood, that it is there and that it is enough.

A further aspect in the work of the Blood is toward Satan, whose most strategic activity today is as the **"accuser of the brethren."** (Revelation 12:10) The Blood operates against Satan by putting God on the side of man. The Fall brought about a state of affairs in man which gave Satan a footing within him, with the result that God was compelled to withdraw Himself. Man is now outside the garden – beyond the reach of the glory of God (Romans 3:23) – because he is "inwardly' estranged from God. Because man has sinned, there is that in him now which, until it is removed, renders God morally unable to defend him. But the Blood removes that barrier, and restores man to God and God to man. How gracious is our God! Man has been restored to favor now, and because God is on his side, man can face Satan without fear.

Remember, I John 4:4 says, **"...greater is he that is in you,** (God) **than he that is in the world** (Satan)."

John says in his first epistle that, *"The Blood of Jesus His Son cleanses us from every sin."* (1 John 1:7) What does this mean? This is a marvelous thing! God is in the light, and as we walk in the light with Him, everything (both good and bad) is exposed and open to that light, so that God can see it all – and yet the Blood is able to cleanse away every sin! Here, God is in the light, and I too am in the light, and there the precious Blood cleanses me from every sin. The Blood is all-sufficient for this!

Some of us, oppressed by our own weakness, may at times have been tempted to think that there are sins which are unforgivable. Let us remember the Word: *"The Blood of Jesus Christ His Son cleanses us from every sin."* Big sins, small sins, sins which may seem really gross, and sins which appear to be not so bad. Sins for which I think I can be forgiven, and sins which seem unforgivable. Yes, all sins, conscious or unconscious, old or new, remembered or forgotten, are included in those words: "every sin." The Word says, *"The Blood of Jesus Christ His Son cleanses us from every sin,"* and it does so because in the first place it satisfies God.

Since God, seeing all sins in the light, can forgive them on the basis of the Blood, what ground of accusation has Satan? Satan may accuse us before Him, but, *"If God is for us, who is against us?"* (Romans 8:31) God points him to the Blood of His dear Son. It is the all-sufficient answer for which Satan has no appeal.

"Who shall lay anything to the charge of God's elect? It is God that justifies; who is he that shall condemn? It is Christ Jesus that died, yea rather, that was raised from the dead, who is at the right hand of God, who also makes intercession for us." (Romans 8:33-34) Thus God answers every challenge.

So here again our need is to recognize the absolute sufficiency of the precious Blood. *"Christ having come a high priest ... through His own blood, entered in once for all into the holy place, having obtained eternal redemption."* (Hebrews 9:11-12) He was our Redeemer *once*. He has been High Priest and Advocate for 2,000 years. He stands there in the presence of God, and *"He is the propitiation for our sins."* (1 John 2:1-2) Note the words of Hebrews 9:14; *"How much more shall the blood of Christ ... cleanse your conscience."* They underline the sufficiency of His ministry. <u>It is enough for God.</u>

What then should be our attitude toward Satan? This is important, for he accuses us not only before God, but in our own conscience also. Satan's argument is: "You have sinned, and you keep on sinning. You are weak, and God can have nothing more to do with you." Our temptation is to look within and in self-defense try to find – in ourselves, our feelings, or our behavior – some ground in which to believe that Satan is wrong. On the other hand, we are tempted to admit our helplessness and, going to the other extreme, give in to depression and despair. Thus, accusation becomes one of the greatest and most effective of Satan's weapons. He points to our sins and seeks to charge us with them before God, and if we accept his accusations we are crushed on the spot!

Now, think about this: The reason why we readily accept his accusations is that we are still hoping to hang onto some righteousness of our own! The premise of our expectation is faulty. Satan has succeeded in making us look in the wrong direction. Thereby he wins his point, rendering us hopeless! But, if we have learned to have no confidence in the flesh, we will be aware that we sin, for the very nature of the flesh is to sin. In order to see this, we have to come to grips with our true sinful nature and see how helpless we are when we hope to find some expectation of righteousness in ourselves. Therefore, when Satan comes along and accuses us, we fall to pieces.

God is well able to deal with our sins; but He cannot deal with a man under accusation, because such a man is not trusting in the Blood. The Blood speaks of God's grace, but man is listening to Satan. Christ is our Advocate, but we, the accused, side with the accuser. We have not yet realized that we are not worthy of anything but death; that, as we shall shortly see, we are only fit to be crucified, anyway. We have not realized that it is Jesus alone Who can answer the accuser, and that by His precious Blood He has already done so.

Our salvation lies in looking away to the Lord Jesus and in seeing that the Blood of the Lamb has met the whole situation created by our sins and has taken care of it. That is the sure foundation on which we stand. Never should we try to answer Satan with our good conduct, but always with the Blood. Yes, we are sinful, but – praise God! – the Blood cleanses us from every sin! God looks upon the Blood whereby His Son has refuted Satan's charge, and Satan has no more grounds for attack. Our faith in the precious Blood and our refusal to be moved from that position can alone silence his charges and put him to flight.

"Who shall lay any thing to the charge of God's elect? It is God that justifies. Who is he that condemns? It is Christ that died, yea rather, that is risen again, who is even at the right hand of God, who also makes intercession for us." (Romans 8:33-34) And so it will be, right on to the end: *"And they overcame him by the blood of the Lamb, and by the word of their testimony, and they loved not their lives unto the death."* (Revelation 12:11)

Oh, what emancipation it would be if we saw more of the value in God's eyes of the precious Blood of His dear Son!

Chapter Thirteen
THE REVELATION OF
THE CROSS OF CHRIST

When God's light first shines into my heart, my one cry is for forgiveness because I realize I have committed sins before Him. However, after I have received forgiveness of *sins*, I then make a new discovery – namely, the discovery of *sin* – a power within that draws me to sin. What happened! I thought I was done with sin! When that power breaks out, I commit sins. I may seek and receive forgiveness, but then it happens once more. So life goes on in a vicious circle of sinning and being forgiven and then sinning again. I appreciate the blessed fact of God's forgiveness, but I want something more than that: I want deliverance. *I need forgiveness for what I have done, but I need also deliverance from what I am!* Then, by God's grace, I found this verse in Romans 6:6: *"Knowing this, that our old man was crucified with [Him], that the body of sin might be annulled, so that we no longer serve sin."* (*Interlinear Bible – Greek/English*) Thank God! He has made a way to deliver me!

We have seen that Romans, Chapters 1 to 8, falls into two sections, and in the first section we are shown that the Blood deals with what we have *done*, while in the second we shall see that the Cross deals with what we *are*. So, we need also the Cross for deliverance. We have dealt briefly above with the first of these two and we shall move on now to the second; but, before that, we will look at some further distinctions.

It is generally understood that "the Cross" signifies the entire redemptive work accomplished historically in the death, resurrection and ascension of the Lord Jesus Himself. *"In being found in fashion as a man, he humbled himself, and became obedient unto death, even the death of the Cross. Wherefore God also has highly exalted him, and given him a name which is above every name."* (Philippians 2:8-9)

However, in a broader sense, the union of believers with Him was achieved through grace. *"Therefore we are buried with him by baptism into death; that like as Christ was raised up from the dead by the glory of the Father, even so we also should walk in newness of life." "Even when we were dead in sins [He] hath quickened us together with Christ, (by grace ye are saved); and hath raised us up together, and made us sit together in heavenly places in Christ Jesus."* (Romans 6:4; Ephesians 2:5-6 KJV) Clearly in that use of the term, the operation of "the Blood" in relation to the forgiveness of sins (as dealt with earlier) is, from God's viewpoint, included as a part of the work of the Cross.

So we see that objectively that the Blood deals with our sins (plural). The Lord Jesus has borne them on the Cross for us as our Substitute and has thereby obtained for us forgiveness, justification and reconciliation! But we must now go a step further in the plan of God to understand how He deals with the sin (singular) principle in us, and solves the problem of our nature to repeatedly sin. **The Blood can wash away my sins, but it cannot wash away my "old man."** It needs the Cross to crucify me! The Blood deals with the sins, but the Cross must deal with the sinner.

You will scarcely find the "sinner" in the first four chapters of Romans. This is because there the sinner himself is not mainly in view, but rather the sins he has committed. The word "sinner" first comes into prominence only in Chapter 5, and it is important to notice how the sinner is there introduced. In that chapter, a sinner is said to be one because he is born a sinner; not because he has committed sins. The distinction is important. It is true that when a Christian wants to convince someone that they are a sinner, he will often use the favorite verse, Romans 3:23, where it says that *"all have sinned,"* but this use of the verse is not strictly justified by the Scriptures. Those who so use it are in danger of arguing the wrong way around, for the teaching of Romans is not that we are sinners because we commit sins, but that we sin because we are sinners. As we said before, we are sinners by constitution rather than by action. As Romans 5:19 expresses it: *"Through one man's disobedience the many were made (or 'constituted') sinners."*

How were we constituted sinners? By Adam's disobedience. We do not become sinners by what we have done, but because of what Adam has done and has become. Romans 3 draws our attention to what we have done – *"all have sinned"* – but it is nevertheless not because we have sinned that we become sinners.

It is true that one who sins is a sinner, but the fact that he sins is merely the evidence that he is already a sinner; it is not the cause. But, it is equally true that one who does not seem to sin, if he is of Adam's race, is a sinner, too, and in need of redemption. Therefore, we agree with Scripture – everyone is a sinner. We sometimes think that if only we had not committed certain sins all would be well; but the trouble lies far deeper than in what we do: it lies in what we are. A Mexican may be born in America and unable to speak Spanish at all, but he is still a Mexican in spite of this, because he was born a Mexican! It is birth that counts. So I am a sinner because I am born in Adam. It is a matter not of my behavior but of my heredity, my parentage. I am not a sinner because I sin, but I sin because I come of the wrong stock. I sin because I am a sinner.

Many of us think that what we have done is very bad, but that we ourselves are not so bad. God is taking pains to show us that we ourselves are wrong, fundamentally wrong. The root trouble is the sinner; he must be dealt with. Our sins are dealt with by the Blood, but we ourselves are dealt with by the Cross. The Blood procures our pardon for what we have done; the Cross procures our deliverance from what we are, sinners, who by nature repeatedly sin.

In Romans 5:12-21 we are not only told something about Adam; we are told also about the Lord Jesus. *"As through the one man's disobedience the many were made sinners, even so through the obedience of the One shall the many be made righteous."* In Adam we receive everything that is of Adam; in Christ we receive everything that is of Christ.

Now, this is the exact meaning of "in Christ." Abraham, as the head of the family of faith, includes the whole family in himself. (Hebrews 7) When he offered to Melchizedek a tithe of his spoils, the whole family offered "in him" to Melchizedek. They did not offer separately as individuals, but they were *in him*, and therefore in making his offering he included with himself all his seed.

So we are presented with a new possibility. In Adam all was lost. Through the disobedience of one man we were all constituted sinners. By him sin entered, and death through sin, and throughout the human race sin has reigned unto death from that day on. But now a ray of light is cast upon the scene! Through the obedience of Another we may be constituted righteous! *"Where sin abounded grace did much more abound, and as sin reigned unto death, even so may grace reign through righteousness into eternal life by Jesus Christ our Lord."* (Romans 5:20-21) Our despair is in Adam; our hope is in Christ.

All our sins are upon Jesus. Isaiah 53:6 says: *"We all like sheep have gone astray; each of us has turned to his own way, and Jehovah has caused the iniquity of us all to fall on Him."* The words "fall on" here can also be translated as "placed upon." All our sins have been placed upon Jesus. An accountant once said that this is like transferring a bank account. Originally, sin was in your account. Now it has been transferred to the account of Jesus Christ. Amazing! God has caused the iniquity of us all to be placed on Him.

Paul in his letter to the Romans opens Chapter 6 with this question: *"Shall we continue in sin?"* Then he exclaims: *"God forbid!"* How could a holy God be satisfied to have unholy, sin-infested children? And so *"...how shall we any longer live therein?"* (Romans 6:1-2) We were born sinners; how then can we cut off our sinful heredity? Being that we were born in Adam, how can we get out of Adam? There is only one way. As we said earlier, since we came in by birth we must go out by death. To do away with our sinfulness we must do away with our life! Bondage to sin came by birth; deliverance from sin comes by death – and it is just this way of escape that God has provided. Death is the secret of emancipation! *"We ... died to sin."* (Romans 6:2)

But how do we die? Some of us have tried very hard to get rid of this sinful life, but we have found this impossible. What are we supposed to do? Simply recognize that God has dealt with us in Christ! This is summed up in Paul's next statement: *"All we who were baptized into Christ Jesus were baptized into His death."* (Romans 6:3) What is baptism? It is your emancipation from the world! It frees you from the brotherhood to which you once belonged. The world knew that you were one with it, but the moment you were baptized, it immediately became aware of the fact that you were finished with it. Before baptism, you knew you had eternal life because you "believed" in Jesus Christ as the Son of God; after baptism, you knew you were saved. Now, everyone recognizes that you are the Lord's, for you belong to Him. *"He that believeth and is baptized shall be saved; but he that disbelieveth shall be condemned."* (Mark 16:16 KJV)

Baptism is a public announcement that declares, "I have come out of the world." The Bible tells us that after our co-crucifixion with Christ we need to buried with Him, too. The biblical meaning of baptism is not only a cleansing, but a burial. We must be baptized because in doing so we testify to the fact that we believe we have died. Hence, we ask someone to bury us beneath the water of baptism. This confirms our belief that we have died. Really, anyone who does not believe that he is dead should not be baptized – for this would be a burying him alive! He who is baptized must believe he was crucified with Christ. So, how do you express your faith? How do you testify to the completed work of Christ? Through baptism. When you are buried in the water and are baptized, you express your faith (1) in the cleansing of your sins through the blood of Christ, and (2) in the co-crucifixion of your old man with Christ on the Cross. You believe the fact; therefore, you receive baptism to prove you are now cleansed and dead.

Now, if God has dealt with us "in Christ Jesus" on the Cross, then we have got to be in Him for this to become effective, but how is this possible? How are we to "get into" Christ? Here again God solves our problem. We have, in fact, no way of getting in, but, what is more important, we need not try, for we are already *in!* What we could not do for ourselves, God has done for us! He has put us in Christ.

One of the best verses in the whole New Testament is found in 1 Corinthians 1:30: *"Ye are in Christ."* How? *"Of Him (that is, "of God") are ye in Christ."* Praise God! This is not left up to us. God has planned it; and He has not only planned it, but He has also performed it. *"Of Him are ye in Christ Jesus."* It is a divine act, and it is already accomplished.

Now if this is true, certain things follow. In the illustration from Hebrews 7 which we considered above, we saw that "in Abraham" all Israel – and therefore Levi who was not yet born – offered tithes to Melchizedek. They did not offer separately and individually, but they were *in Abraham* when he offered his tithes, and his offering included all his seed. This, then is a true figure of ourselves as "in Christ." When the Lord Jesus was on the Cross, **all of us died** – not individually, for we had not yet been born – but, being *in Him*, we died. *"One died for all, therefore all died."* (2 Corinthians 5:14) When he was crucified on the Cross, all of us were crucified there with him!

A good example of our being "in Christ" on the Cross as well as in His Resurrection and Ascension, is a very simple illustration for this divine truth. Imagine a piece of paper being put into a small book. Now, we have two identities: the book and the paper. Then, the book is mailed, say from New York to California. The paper is not mailed, but the paper has been put in the book. Then where is the paper? Can the book go to California and the paper remain in New York? Can the paper have a separate destiny from the book? No! Where the book goes, the paper goes. If I drop the book in the river, the paper goes too, and if I quickly take it out again I recover the paper also. Whatever experience the book goes through, the paper goes through with it, for it is still there in the book.

"Of Him are ye in Christ Jesus." The Lord God Himself has put us in Christ, and in His dealing with Christ, He has dealt with the whole human race. Our destiny is bound up with His. What He has gone through we have gone through, for to be "in Christ" is to have been identified with Him in both His death and Resurrection. He was crucified: then what about us? Must we ask God to crucify us also? Never! When Christ was crucified, we were crucified; and His crucifixion is past, therefore ours cannot be future. All the references to it are in the Greek *aorist,* which is the "once-for-all" tense, the "eternal past" tense. (See: Romans 6:6; Galatians 2:20; 5:24; 6:14) And just as no man could ever commit suicide by crucifixion, for it is a physical impossibility to do so, so also, in spiritual terms, God does not require us to crucify ourselves. We were crucified when Christ was crucified, for God put us there in

Him. That we have died in Christ is not merely a doctrinal position, it is an eternal and indisputable fact!

The Lord Jesus, when He died on the Cross, shed His Blood, thus giving His sinless life to atone for our sin and to satisfy the righteousness and holiness of God. To do so was the prerogative of the Son of God alone. No man could have a share in that. The Scripture has never told us that we shed our blood with Christ. In His atoning work before God, He acted alone; no other could have a part. But the Lord did not die only to shed His Blood: He died so that we might die. He died as our Representative. In His death He included you and me. *"I have been crucified with Christ; it is no longer I who live, but Christ lives in me; and the life which I now live in the flesh I live by faith in the Son of God, who loved me and gave Himself for me."* (Galatians 2:20)

The death of the Lord Jesus is inclusive. The resurrection of the Lord Jesus is likewise inclusive. We have looked at the first chapter of 1 Corinthians to establish the fact that we are "in Christ Jesus." Later in this same letter, 1 Corinthians 15:45-47, two remarkable names or titles are used of the Lord Jesus. He is spoken of there as "the last Adam" and also "the second Man." Scripture does not refer to Him as the second Adam but as "the last Adam"; nor does it refer to Him as the last Man, but as "the second Man." The distinction is to be emphasized, for it enshrines a truth of great value.

As the last Adam, Christ is the sum total of Humanity; as the second Man He is the head of a new race. So we have here two unions, the one relating to His death and the other to His resurrection. In the first place His union with the race as "the last Adam" began historically at Bethlehem and ended at the Cross and the tomb. In it He gathered up into Himself all that was in Adam and took it to judgment and death. In the second place, our union with Him as "the second Man" begins in Resurrection and ends in Eternity. In other words, it never ends! Now, in having His death done away with, the first man (Adam) in whom God's purpose was frustrated, He rose again as Head of a new race of men, in whom that purpose will in time be fully realized.

When therefore the Lord Jesus was crucified on the Cross, He was crucified as the last Adam. All that was in the first Adam (sin and all) was gathered up and done away with in Him. We were included there! As the last Adam He wiped out the old race; as the second Man (Jesus Christ) He brings in the new race. It is in His resurrection that He stands forth as the second Man, and there, too, we are included. *"For if we have become united with Him by the likeness of His death, we shall be also by the likeness of His resurrection."* (Romans 6:5)

We died in Him as the last Adam; we live in Him as the second Man. The Cross is thus the mighty act of God which translated us from Adam to Christ.

Chapter Fourteen
THE REVELATION OF GOD'S RIGHTEOUSNESS

God loves us more that we can ever imagine! He made the universe and everything in it, and there is no limit to His power and wisdom. Why is it, then – in order for Him to forgive our sins and grant us salvation – that His Son had to step down and become a man (a perfectly holy Man in God's sight)? And why did He need to take all the sins of the world on Himself to become a living sacrifice, and be crucified on a Roman Cross? Our head knowledge knows that God loves us, but this does not make any sense. Why would God even consider doing this to His Son?

For God to forgive and save man would have been easy, but it was impossible to do without breaking His own law! "Righteousness" is God's requirement, His way, and His method. God could not break His own law to save us. Take the sin of man and the love of God. Bring them together regarding man's salvation. Add the righteousness of God to these two, and try to figure out a way to save mankind and you'll find it becomes the most difficult task on the whole earth! This impossible assignment was accomplished by God through the work of redemption by the Lord Jesus. If there could have been love without righteousness, the Lord Jesus would not have needed to come to earth, and the Cross would have been unnecessary. Without the need for righteousness, God could have saved us any way He chose. This is where God's holiness is manifested. In fact, it ought to be an accurate yardstick to show us how much God hates sin!

Death is the rightful penalty for sin (Romans 5:12), and since men are guilty of it, they must die. God cannot overlook it and forsake righteousness in order to dispense grace. He cannot save men without punishing sin. Although He wants to save men, His righteousness demands that the price be paid. Only a sinless God could come, take on our load of guilt, and bear the consequence of our sin. He had to die. But our all-wise, all-powerful God cannot die! That is why for Him to bear the judgment of man's sins against Him, He had to take on the body of a man. Our God, though desirous of saving us, cannot be unrighteous. He, therefore, gave us His Son, who – incarnated as a man – came into the world to receive in Himself as a man the penalty of sins which was death on the Cross for mankind.

Thus, sin can be judged – and men can be saved! How ingenious of God! Who on earth could have come up with such a plan? Furthermore, it is men who sin, so it must be a man who receives its penalty. Even if God could die, He would die in vain, for it is men and not God who sin. This is another reason why God had to become man. Mankind has sinned, therefore the *"one mediator ... between God and men" must be "himself man, [even] Jesus Christ."* (1 Timothy 2:5) Christ is the unique man, in that He included all mankind in Himself and received the penalty of sin.

Nevertheless, although He is God, Jesus became truly man. To be absolutely clear about this, please note: He is in such complete union with men that His death is recognized as the death of all mankind! Because the Lord Jesus had no sin, He should not have had to die. Therefore, His death can be called "substitutionary." We have sinned, and hence we should be punished; but we have the Cross to present to God as our effective defense. Before God granted us the Cross, we would have had no alibi if He had decided to punish us! But since He has given us the Cross, He cannot help but forgive our sins and accept us. Let us remember that upon our once having the Cross, our salvation is based on the "righteousness" of God – this is, by definition, "to be in right standing with God." **Without** the Cross none can be saved, since God cannot be *un*righteous. But **with** the Cross, God has committed Himself to save us, and this He accomplished within the Law.

God, then, had to propound a way by which He could forgive us – and at the same time satisfy His own right-eousness. He must be able to keep His Law, even as He forgives us. This is called "the grace of God." God's grace means that all the laws of God are still kept intact and yet we may be saved. Salvation implies that men can be saved while, simultaneously, God remains righteous. He leaves no ground for any to criticize. He leaves us speechless! Furthermore, He must save us in such a way that the devil's mouth, too, is rendered speechless – he cannot accuse God of being *un*righteous.

Lastly, He must save us to the extent that He Himself has no more to say. The salvation of God must not only look right in the eyes of men and of the adversary, but in His own sight as well. As stated earlier, for God to save us was not at all difficult, but to save **justly** was quite another matter. The Bible affirms that in saving men God has so worked that neither the saved nor the unsaved, neither the devil nor even God Himself, has any valid complaint. This is called "salva-tion," which will be discussed in more detail later. Salvation is "God saving people with His righteousness;" and this is God's masterpiece!

What, then, is our right standing? All Christians must understand this. We ought to know that in providing for our salvation, God solved the problem of our justification as well as sin. Through righteousness, God has forgiven our sins, and He has also prepared justification for us by which we can always come to Him. The Word of God tells us that our righteousness is Christ – the Lord Jesus Himself. **"But of (God) are ye in Christ Jesus, who was made unto us wisdom from God, and righteousness and sanctification,** *and redemption."* (1Corinthians 1:30) Essentially, God has made Christ our righteousness, but what does that mean?

The Bible, from its beginning to its end, tells us that we do not become righteous by His righteousness. Our right standing before God is only because of Christ Himself. It is wrong to consider Christ's righteousness as our own, since what's His cannot be ours. It is **Christ Himself** who is our righteousness which He lived out while on earth. It is His personal standing before God – exclusively His and absolutely unrelated to us. It is for this reason that the Word of God never says that we are "in Jesus" – instead we are said to be "in Christ." In being "Jesus" He is still "the seed' of Abraham; He has yet to die and be buried to bring forth "much fruit" (many grains). Only since the Lord Jesus has died are we now those fruits, those many grains. Our union with Christ began at His death, not His birth. *Calvary* is where we are united with Him; at Bethlehem there is no such union. Before Calvary, we could see Christ's righteousness; it was solely His. Since Calvary, we can now "share" in His righteousness in our "own" right standing before God because of Christ Himself.

Let's look at this illustration. Imagine that we owe God $1,000,000, but we have no way to repay it. Because He loves us, He cannot ask us to pay Him back. But because He is righteous, He will not tell us that we have no need to repay at all. For us to pay Him back is impossible. Yet for God to release us from our obligation would be unjust. Thank and praise Him that He has come to give us the "money," that we can pay back what we owe Him! The collector is God, and the payer is also God. Without collecting, there is no righteousness; but if we are made to pay, there is no love. Now, God Himself is the collector; therefore, righteousness is maintained. And God Himself is also the payer; therefore, love is maintained. Hallelujah! The collector is the payer! This is the biblical meaning of redemption from sins.

Therefore, before the Lord Jesus came to the earth and was crucified on the Cross, it would have been perfectly all right for God to refuse to save us. Had God not given us His Son, all we could have said was that God did not love us. We could say nothing more. But because He has indeed given us His Son and put our sins upon Him that we might be redeemed from them, God can do no less than forgive us when we come to Him through the blood of the Lord Jesus and through His work.

Hallelujah! God has to forgive our sins! If you come to God through Jesus Christ, God is bound to forgive you. It was love that brought His Son to the Cross, but it was righteousness that caused God to forgive our sins.

Today, some say that if God loved us, He could forgive us without judgment. That would be grace reigning without righteousness. But grace is reigning through it. Grace needs the justifying work of Calvary before it can reign. Today, our receiving of grace is based solely upon God's righteousness. Our sins are forgiven after they are dealt with on the Cross. When we see the Cross, it signifies that this is God's righteousness and God's grace. To God, the Cross is righteousness; to us, it is grace. Thank and praise the Lord! The Cross has solved the problem of sin!

God's redemption reveals His righteousness which is freely given to all who believe! The Bible tells us that our right standing is in Christ, making us God's righteousness. It shows us that a Christian has two garments: one is the Lord Jesus, for He is our robe, our righteousness; the other is the bright and pure fine linen of Revelation 19:8*: "For the fine linen is the righteous acts of the saints."* All the good conduct of a Christian – all his outward righteousness – comes from grace as a result of the working of the Holy Spirit in him; it is not something which he has naturally. As we approach God we are not naked, because we are clothed with Christ who is our righteousness. However, The Revelation tells us that, as we appear before the judgment seat of

Christ, we must bring our own righteousness, that which is called "the righteousness of the saints" (see also 2 Corinthians 5:10, 1 Corinthians 4:5), and this will be discussed at a later time.

One name in the Old Testament is most precious: *"Jehovah our righteousness."* (Jeremiah 23:6, 33:16) This literally means that Jehovah is our righteousness; therefore it is not our *conduct* that makes us righteous. May God give us revelation to see the Gospel, even the foundation of the Gospel. As we come to God, Christ – not our conduct – is our righteousness. We come to God through Christ.

There is nothing more immoveable or rock solid than this!

Chapter Fifteen
CHRIST'S RESURRECTION
AND OUR JUSTIFICATION

What proof do we have that Christ's death on the Cross has saved us from our sins? For that matter, how do we know that the Lord's work of redemption is acceptable to God the Father, and if so, what is the evidence? Consider this! God raised up the Lord Jesus from the dead as proof that the work of redemption had been accomplished! God has justified and approved it! Now He is satisfied.

The resurrection of the Lord represents God's approval on the work and death of the Lord Jesus. Man's problem with sin is now officially solved. The proof that we are fully redeemed from our sins is exhibited by the Lord Jesus' resurrection. It shows us that the Cross was *entirely adequate* and resurrection was approved.

The Lord Jesus went through death for us. Remember, even though He was without sin, He went through the punishment of the Law and the wrath of God toward us. *"Christ has redeemed us from the curse of the law, being made a curse for us...."* (Galatians 3:13) Then, on the Cross before He died, Jesus clearly said, "It is finished!" (John 19:30) We might ask, "What is finished?" His life? His earthly life, yes. But not only this – the eternal purpose of redemption was accomplished! *Finished!*

However, if the Lord Jesus had not returned from the dead, we would have no grounds to believe that His work was finished. We wouldn't know if God had accepted the Lord's sacrifice. For this reason, the Lord Jesus must be resurrected. Praise His Name! He did, and we are justified!

His resurrection proves that our sin debt has been fully paid. Romans 4:25 says, *"Who was delivered for our offenses and was raised for our justification."* What does it mean to be "justified?" To make it simple, the word "justified" can be put another way: "Just as if I had never sinned." This means that Jesus was delivered to the Cross for our sins and was resurrected for our justification. Therefore, the resurrection of the Lord Jesus is our proof of justification before God.

This verse from Romans indicates two things:

(1) That the Lord Jesus died to bear our sins, and that through His death He received their penalty that we might be forgiven. This means that even though we have sinned – if we have repented and believed in the saving power of Christ – our sins are forgiven by God.

But (2), that His resurrection is for our justification. Here it shows that we have no sin because God declares us to be without sin. Yet how can this be? On the basis of the death of our Lord Jesus Christ we have received forgiveness, and are justified by God. What a beautiful concept! I remember hearing that "forgiveness is the fragrance that a violet sheds on the heel that crushes it!" How merciful and God-like is this virtue called forgiveness!

Resurrection causes us to have a new relationship with God. Due to the resurrection of the Lord Jesus, we now stand before God on a new basis and in a new position. Death and resurrection are closely joined; therefore forgiveness and justification are tightly entwined. Because of the death of the Lord Jesus, a Christian senses in his spirit that his sins have been borne away by the Lord, judged in Christ, and forgiven by God. Because of the resurrection, he knows that he is no longer a "forgiven, miserable prisoner," but a fully-accepted "child of God." Resurrection means that all in the past is dead. Whatever is of sin and of self has been buried in the tomb, out of sight – nevermore to be seen. The life the Christian now has is altogether new! We believe daily that we are accepted in Christ even as Christ is accepted by the Father. As God is pleased with Christ, so He is pleased with us – for we are joined to Him in both His death and resurrection.

In Romans, Chapter 3, Paul tells us that we are justified freely through the blood of the Lord Jesus. From the beginning, in the Garden of Eden, blood was the only atonement God recognized for sin. Later, blood from an unblemished bull or goat had to be repeated, over and over again. Now, we can say that Jesus has died, once and for all, for us and for our sins. Humanly speaking, we still cannot calculate the value of the Lord's work on the Cross.

However, God knows the value of the blood, as is recorded Exodus 12:7. There, the blood was put on the *outside* of the house, on the two posts and the lintel of the door, so God and the Angel of Death could see it, but the occupants of the house could not. Also, in Leviticus 16:14-15 it was brought into the Holy of Holies and put in the place of atonement for sin. It was there only for God to see. And, later, when God had seen the blood of His Son, the perfect and final sacrifice, resurrection was His stamp of approval for our justification.

Therefore, because God saw that that the work of the Lord had fulfilled all His righteous requirements, everyone who comes to God in faith is now justified. He knew that we would be what Jesus called "little faiths." He knew that we would doubt that His gift of His Son would suffer judgment and accomplish redemption for us. He knew we would doubt that anyone who received His Son would be justified. This is why He resurrected His Son from the dead to be a proof of our justification.

An example of this proof might be this: As far as my creditor (bank) is concerned, the time a debt is settled is when he sees the money. But for me, it is settled when I see the receipt. My creditor only looks at the money, and I only look at the receipt. God's eyes only see the death of the Lord Jesus, and our eyes only see His resurrection. God does not need the resurrection of the Lord as His proof, or as His receipt. God makes the rules, and knows perfectly well that the Lord's death is adequate for redemption. The problem is that we do not comprehend. A receipt is not given to the One who receives the money! A receipt is given to the debtor (mankind). It is written to give debtors peace of mind.

The fact of forgiveness lies in His death (before God). The assurance of forgiveness lies in His resurrection (before man). Death is for God, but resurrection is for us. Death is God's demand, and resurrection is the sinner's demand. ***Death is the solution of sin before God, and resurrection is the removal of doubt in man's heart.*** With Christ's death, the record of sin is erased. With Christ's resurrection, we realize it is the proof of forgiveness and a "not guilty" verdict. Thank the Lord for Jesus' resurrection, because He justifies those who trust in Him before God the Father!

Chapter 16
THE HOLY SPIRIT AND FAITH

The Bible shows us time and again that God is triune – or three in one – the "Holy Trinity" in terms of the Catholic Church. Two thousand years ago, God – in the Person of His Son – put on human flesh. In other words, He was incarnated to become the Christ, or "the anointed One." Now He has put on the Spirit. God, Christ, and the Holy Spirit are all one entity. The Christ who was clothed with flesh was limited geographically. The Christ who is clothed with the Spirit is Omnipresent! Think of it! As such, He can reside in each one of us. Through faith, everyone who desires may obtain Him, and everyone who believes in Him may receive. He is no longer confined by time and space! We can be one with Him wherever we are and whenever we will!

If Christ is not living in the Holy Spirit, our faith is dead and Christianity is a dead religion. If Christ is not in the Spirit, our beliefs are mere teachings and theories, and we possess nothing in reality because nothing can come into us from the Christ in the flesh.

So, then, Christ is in the Holy Spirit. This is explained more fully in the Gospel of John. *"And I will ask the Father, and He will give you another Comforter, that He may be with you forever."* (John 14:16) The Comforter here is understood to be the Holy Spirit. The original word *parakletos* is formed by two roots. The first part, *para,* means "beside." The second part *kletos* carries the idea of help, or succoring, or "one who comes along side." Hence, the word "Comforter" means someone is helping you at your side. It gives the sense of one being near to you, helping, watching over, and sustaining you. In this passage, Jesus is praying the Father to send a Comforter to help and sustain you.

Verse 17 says, *"Even the Spirit of reality, whom the world cannot receive, because it does not behold Him or know Him; but you know Him, because He abides with you and shall be in you."* This Comforter is the Spirit of reality, truth, the Holy Spirit Himself. When we have Him, we have reality.

The Spirit of reality is only available to believers. He has nothing to do with the world. Why does the world not receive Him? For one thing, it is because it does not see Him. When people in the world do not see something, they naturally will not believe it. Secondly, they do not know Him. Also, something unknown usually has difficulty being accepted. The Lord, however, says, *"But you know Him."* Christians know the Holy Spirit because *"He abides with us."*

Even today, the Holy Spirit is always with believers. This is a fact. But notice the phrase after this: *"And shall be in you."* "Shall be" points to a future time. The Lord was saying, "This Holy Spirit is presently *with* you. But a day will come when He will get *inside* of you." Then Verse 18 says, *"I will not leave you as orphans; I am coming to you."*

What is an orphan? It is a child left alone, without the care of a parent. If a child has a parent, all his living, food, clothing, etc., are provided. The parent prepares everything and does everything for him. An orphan, on the other hand, is "on his own." Speaking on an earthly level, he has no home, no one to care for him, and survives only by stealing, begging, and rummaging in garbage cans for food.

On a spiritual level, however, the Lord is saying that He will not leave us as orphans to manage all of our affairs of the spirit alone. Instead, He will come to be our Father, to care for and look after us.

Listen to this: *"Therefore, I say unto you, take no thought for your life, what you shall eat, or what you shall drink; nor yet for your body, what you shall put on. Is not the life more than meat, and the body than raiment? Behold the fowls of the air: for they sow not, neither do they reap, nor gather into barns; yet your Heavenly Father feeds them. Are you not much better than they?"* (Matthew 6:25-26)

So Jesus is saying in this passage that He will ask the Father, and the Father will send a Comforter (the Holy Spirit) to abide in us. This Comforter is the Spirit of Christ Himself who will dwell inside of us and "guide us into all truth" whereby we will be well-cared for. In this way the disciples would no longer remain orphans.

When Jesus Christ was on the earth, the Holy Spirit (the Comforter), lived in Him. Since His death, resurrection, and ascension, Christ lives in the Holy Spirit. When He was with the disciples on earth, the Holy Spirit was with the disciples already, simply because He (the Holy Spirit) was in Christ. By His death and resurrection, Jesus is able to dwell in us now as the Holy Spirit. Therefore, He comes to His disciples by the Spirit, through the Spirit, and in the Spirit.

"Yet a little while and the world beholds Me no longer, but you behold Me; because I live, you also shall live. In that day you will know that I am in My Father, and you in Me, and I in you." (John 14:19-20)

It can be said that the Holy Spirit is now *in* the disciples. But actually it is *Christ* in the disciples, and in every Christian. This union transmits to us everything that God did in Christ and everything that God is through Him. All of His becomes ours. God and man, man and God, become fully mingled into one.

Christ died and rose from the dead for us. But if He did not come to us in the person of the Holy Spirit, salvation could not be accomplished. Christ could not be joined to us. Since He now has taken on a spiritual form, He can freely enter. The Bible says that *"…he who is joined to the Lord is one spirit…."* (1 Corinthians 6:17) It is clear: Christ is in the Spirit.

All of us also have a spirit. When our spirit receives into us this Christ who is in the Spirit, the two become one. This is the beauty of our faith. Without this belief of "regeneration" – our taking into our bodies the very life of God – our religion becomes just another religion with no relevance to our life. Without this, there cannot be an inward salvation.

"And this is the testimony: God has given us eternal life, and this life is in His Son. He who has the Son has life; he who does not have the Son does not have life." (1John 5:11-12)

By faith in God's Word, His work becomes ours by the fellowship of the Holy Spirit. All of the wonderful works of God were accomplished by His Son, Jesus Christ, and translated to us through the power of the Holy Spirit. God has placed all His works in His Word. Whenever man receives God's Word by faith, the Holy Spirit comes and applies all of God's work to him. Here we see how complete the work of the Triune God (Holy Trinity) is.

It is God who has loved us and has purposed the work of redemption.

It is the Son who accomplished the work of redemption.

It is God who placed the work of the Son in the Word, and it is God who communicates to us through the Holy Spirit all the works of the Son contained in the Word.

The Bible tells us clearly that only the Holy Spirit can communicate the Lord's work to us. *"All Scripture is given by inspiration of God, and is profitable for doctrine, for reproof, for correction, for instruction in righteousness: that the man of God may be perfect, thoroughly furnished unto all good works."* (2 Timothy 3:16-17)

This characteristic of the Holy Spirit's work is known as "fellowship" which is the same as "communion."

After the Lord Jesus accomplished all the work, the Holy Spirit came and communicated this to us. If there were only the accomplished work of the Lord Jesus without the fellowshipping work of the Holy Spirit, it would still be without benefit to us.

Without the Father, man cannot be saved.

Without the Son, man cannot be saved.

Likewise, without the Holy Spirit, man cannot be saved.

Although there is the work of the Father and the Son, there is still the need of the Holy Spirit to communicate these works to us. The only thing we need to do in order for the Holy Spirit to work in us is to believe in the Word, Jesus Christ, the Son of God. Man is justified before God only by faith, not by works. Listen to Paul as he writes to the Galatians, Chapter 2, Verse 16: *"Knowing that a man is not justified by the works of the law, but by the faith of Jesus Christ ... for by the works of the law shall no flesh be justified."*

But what is faith? Amazingly, the word "faith" appears 150 times in the New Testament and even more in the Old Testament, but its definition is given only once. Only in one verse – Hebrews 11:1 – and here it gives us a unique explanation of faith. *"Faith is the assurance of things hoped for, a conviction of things not seen."* (ASV)

Another translation of this verse is from J. N. Darby, who translated the word "assurance" to mean "substantiating." This is the ability which enables us to recognize a substance. For example, when we see a board, we realize that its substance is wood. Or, after looking at it, we are able to tell that the substance covering it is paint. This ability is the substantiating power.

The world around us is composed of myriads of objects of various colors, shapes, sounds, and smells. We communicate with them through our five senses. If a man were deprived of these, it would be extremely difficult for anything from the outside world to come into him.

Take vision, for instance. There is a whole spectrum of colors in the world around us. But if a man is blind, he cannot receive these colors into himself. He cannot appreciate their beauty, for he lacks the ability to substantiate the colors.

If you tell him that snow is beautiful, he will ask, "Why is it so beautiful?"

If you answer that the whiteness is what makes it attractive, he will say, "What is white anyway?"

And if you say that white is opposite of black, he will answer, "I do not know what black is like." There are all kinds of colors in the world. But they can only come into us through the substantiating ability of our eyes. Those without the sense of sight cannot see.

Sounds around us require our being able to hear. Our sense of hearing is required for us to perceive sound. If we are deaf, sound has no effect on us. Then there are some things that call for our tasting or smelling faculties.

The function of our five senses is to transfer all the objective faculties into us to become our subjective experience. If we do not have these five senses, all the outside substances will remain outside of us; they will never be of use to us. There will be forever a barrier between the two sides. The work that the five senses do is a work of substantiating.

God uses the word "substantiating" to show us what faith means. When it comes to spiritual matters, faith comes into action. Faith is the organ whereby we substantiate everything spiritual into us. Without it, every spiritual matter is a nonentity. This is why the Bible calls faith the "substantiation of things hoped for."

Are spiritual matters real or not? You cannot ascertain them by your five senses. God has put us in Christ; we are crucified with Him. All our sins were borne by Him. Today, Christ is resurrected and is in the Holy Spirit. But can we substantiate any of these facts with our five senses? They are useless in this respect. When it comes to these matters, the eyes are blind, the ears deaf, and all the senses dull. If we merely exercise our five senses, we have to conclude that God does not exist.

In the early days of space exploration, Russia sent up a cosmonaut who declared, "God is not here. I do not see God." (*) He was backing up the teachings of Karl Marx, who proclaimed that there was no God. Therefore, if we look only to what our five senses can verify, we will agree that there is no Christ, and that neither forgiveness of sins nor redemption of sinners is substantial, that there is no such thing as a new life, and that all spiritual matters are mere fantasies. The fact is that the substance is there, but the substantiating ability is missing.

Suppose a blind man stands up and says, "There is no such thing as color. All the beautiful sights and scenes that people talk about are just illusions." You would not be surprised at hearing this said by a blind man. You realize that he lacks the ability of seeing. To him, all those things are honestly nonexistent. His theory is the theory of the blind. Only the blind can approve it and justify it.

There are many people in the world who would criticize others, saying, "Listen to all this talk about spiritual things, about forgiveness of sins by Christ, resurrection, and the receiving of a new life. They are just a bunch of empty words."

The fact is that spiritual matters *do* exist, but these people lack faith. They are blind in regard to things of the Spirit. Without faith, every spiritual matter is darkness to them. Faith makes everything spiritually real and clear.

The material world is real, and so is the spiritual world. However, you need a special sense to see and hear in the spiritual world. This sense is the faith previously mentioned. As said before, "...faith is the substantiation of things hoped for, the conviction (proof) of things not seen." Though they are unseen, they are manifested to us in a tangible way. How can a seemingly abstract spiritual entity be substantiated in us? It is by no other way than by faith. Do we have this faith? If we do, then all these will become real.

The five senses substantiate everything to us in the physical world.

Faith is the faculty which substantiates everything in the spiritual world. It is a "sixth" sense in addition to our other five. The question is, "Are we are exercising it?"

My beautiful wife is sitting in front of me here in the room. She becomes real to me through my eyes. However, I can testify to you that the Christ within me is more real than my wife! Not only is His indwelling Holy Spirit a reality; His redemption, His crucifixion of my old man, and my resurrection with Him are also real. I am surer of them than I am of my wife. Within me there is an ability which enables me to perceive all of the above. They are undeniable and certain. Not only I, but countless other Christians have seen them. They are being made real by the unique sense of faith.

God has prepared and accomplished everything in Christ. He has also put Christ into the Holy Spirit so that everyone can henceforth enjoy Him anywhere, anytime. All that it takes is for mankind to receive Him. But how does one go about receiving Him? By faith. Faith is the receiving. When man believes, he receives everything of Christ into himself.

Actually, the five senses also receive. The ears receive sound through hearing, and the eyes receive color through seeing. By constant contact with the outside world, the five senses receive everything into the inside world of our body.

Faith is then an act of receiving. Christ has shed His blood to take away our sins. When we believe, this becomes real to us. God has put us into the death of Christ. By faith this solution of the old man is received into us. Other facts such as His resurrection and the initiation of a new life are all received by faith, all through the power of the Holy Spirit. When we believe in God's Word and works, they come into us. This is the function of faith.

Because the Lord Jesus died on the Cross, I have received forgiveness of sins; because He arose from the dead, I have received new life; because He has been exalted to the right hand of the Father, I have received the outpoured Spirit. All of this is because of Him; nothing is because of me.

As we have said, remission of sins is not based on human merit, but on the Lord's crucifixion; regeneration is not based on human merit, but on the Lord's resurrection; and the outpouring or provision of the Holy Spirit is not based on human merit, but on the Lord's exaltation. The Holy Spirit has not been poured out on us to prove how great we are, but to prove the greatness of the Son of God. The Holy Spirit was poured out on earth to prove what had taken place in Heaven, which was the exaltation of Jesus of Nazareth to the right hand of God. The purpose of Pentecost is to prove the Lordship of Jesus Christ.

The receiving of all such spiritual facts is strictly through the avenue of faith. Faith is a gift from God, and we should pray to receive it. We need faith in His Word. We have to mix His words with our faith. Do not doubt or argue with them. Rather, we should identify ourselves with them and be saved. The place that faith occupies in the Christian belief is paramount. It is nothing other than the receiving of God's testimony for the work of His Son. God has placed it in the Word and has communicated this Word to us by His Holy Spirit. When we believe in it, we are believing in Him.

1 John 5:9 says, *"If we receive the testimony of men, the testimony of God is greater."* What is the characteristic of God's testimony? *"This is the testimony of God that He*

has testified concerning His Son." This means that the Word of God concerns His Son. Verse 10 is important that reads: *"He who believes into the Son of God has the testimony in himself; he who does not believe God has made Him a liar, because he has not believed in the testimony which God has testified concerning His Son."*

Then what does it mean to "believe in God?" It is to believe in the words God has spoken, the testimony He has made concerning His Son. Therefore, to believe in God is nothing other than to believe in God's testimony. It is to believe in God *through* His Word – and there is only one way to receive Christ, and that is by faith. The minute we believe in Him, His resurrection life comes into us.

Simply put, by faith, when we believe in Christ, everything of Him will be transmitted into us through the power of His Holy Spirit.

(*)   Taken from a sermon by Revelation Roger Fritts, February 11, 2001, Bethesda, MD.

Chapter 17
SALVATION – BY FAITH ALONE

To sum up this book, let me review our premise: We have seen that, through God's infinite love,

1) He created man in the image of Jesus Christ, His Son.
2) God did not want robots, so he gave mankind a free will to love and serve Him.
3) Man failed miserably, disobeying God and thereby infecting the whole human race with sin.
4) Man could not realize that he was useless, unable to please God in the flesh no matter how hard he tried.
5) God had to show man, through His grace and mercy, that He would accomplish everything that He desired by sending His only begotten Son to righteously die on the Cross for our sins and resurrect for us, thereby justifying us and awarding us salvation.
6) This shows us that God loves us beyond our wildest imagination, and now all He asks of us is to BELIEVE in His Son. Grace is God giving something to us, and faith is our receiving something from God. Faith is nothing other than receiving what God has given us through the Holy Spirit. This is absolutely independent from works, otherwise it would not be grace.
7) As has been shown, all those who read the Bible know that the condition for salvation is faith. There is no other qualification. Because man has fallen and is corrupted, his thoughts are sinful, and man's flesh is of the Law, he thinks he must do something before he can be saved. But the Bible shows us that the only condition for our salvation is faith. The New Testament

tells us clearly at least 115 times that when man believes, he is saved, he has eternal life and is justified. In addition, the Bible says that man is justified by faith, or becomes righteous through faith, 35 times. *"What must I do to be saved? ... Believe on the Lord Jesus, and thou shalt be saved."* (Acts 16:30-31)

From this it is clear that the Bible tells us that: Once a man believes, he is saved.

Once a man believes, he has eternal life. (John 3:36)

Once a man believes, he is justified.

Hence, in the entire New Testament, at least 150 times it says that man is saved, justified, and has eternal life *only* through faith. The Gospel of John mentions 86 times that, by faith alone, man receives life, is justified, and does not come into condemnation. Period. It makes no difference who a person is, what he has done, or what he can do. Everything depends on believing. It is clear: *Everything depends on faith.*

What is salvation? It is God saving man out of himself into Himself! Salvation has two facets: a cutting off and a uniting with. What is cut off is self; the uniting is with God. A true spiritual beginning involves release from the animal life and entry into the divine life.

Salvation, then, is to deliver man from his created, fleshly, natural will. Of special importance is that, aside from God giving us a new life, or "the turning over of our will to Him" is the greatest work in salvation. The Gospel is to facilitate the union of our will with God's will. God aims His arrow of salvation not so much at our emotions or our minds, but at our wills – for once the will is saved, the rest of the soul (mind and emotion) are included. Even so noble an entity as the spirit must yield to the rule of the will!

The spirit does not symbolize the whole man, for it is but his means of communication with God. The body cannot stand for man either, because it is only his instrument by which he communicates with the world. But the will embodies man's intention and man's condition (his authentic attitude); therefore, man's will must be united with God's will.

So you can see that our union with the Lord involves two steps: the union of life and the union of will. We are united with Him in life at the time we are regenerated and receive His life. As Christ lives by His Spirit so shall we thereafter live by the Holy Spirit. This is the "bond of life." It indicates that we share one life with God and is an internal union. However, what expresses that life is the will, and this is an external manifestation. These two unions are related and interdependent upon each other. The one of regeneration (our new life) is spontaneous, for this new life is the life of God; but the one of the will is not so simple or spontaneous, because our *will* is clearly our "self" and needs to be cut off.

But what do we do about the keeping of the Law? What about the Ten Commandments given to Moses by God Himself? Is man saved through faith with the keeping of the Law? Absolutely not! And in order to prove this let me ask a question: Why did God give them the Law? I believe that God gave the Israelites the Law, *not for them to keep, but for exposing their sins!* Originally, the Israelites had sins, but they had not yet become *transgressions* (acts of violation of a Law).

God says that the Law is perfect. It is good, righteous, holy, and excellent. (Romans 7:12) However, from Adam to Moses, man had no transgressions although he was full of sin. *"Nevertheless, death reigned from Adam to Moses even over them that had not sinned after the similitude of Adam's transgression...."* (Romans 5:14)

Therefore, God established the Law, not in order that man would not sin, but in order to *expose* man's sins and show them their true condition in God's eyes. *"Before the law was given, sin was in the world. But sin is not taken into account when there is no law ... the law was added so that the trespass might increase."* (Romans 5:13,20a NIV)

Today, we still have the Law. Once a person breaks that Law, he realizes that he has sinned. Therefore, we can say that God gave it to man – not for him to keep – but for him to see that he has sinned! Before the Law, he did not realize that he was a sinner. Now he knows.

The strange thing is that man takes the Law, which is there to prove his sin, to try to prove that he is righteous! He turns it around!

God wants us to know by it that we have sinned, but we want to prove through it that we are righteous.

God wants to show us by it that we are perishing, but we want to prove through keeping the Law that we are saved. Obviously, man does not see himself. His thoughts are full of the Law, but he fails to see that he is corrupt inside and cannot keep it. Man's flesh can never keep or even submit to God's Law.

However, man still seeks out righteousness from the Law and to earn life through a "do-it-myself salvation!" But God uses it to show man that he is helpless and that he must receive salvation through His grace. However, when man sees the ordinances, he tries to earn a little righteousness through them and be saved.

Romans 3:19 says, *"Now we know that whatever things the law says, it speaks to those who are under the law, that every mouth may be stopped and all the world may fall under the judgment of God."* Imagine! Here it says that the Law was given for the purpose of stopping every mouth, so that no one can refute it, and so that everyone will be subject to the judgment of God.

The next verse is a verdict concerning us*: "Because out of the works of the law no flesh shall be justified before Him; for through the law is the clear knowledge of sin."* (Verse 20) Here again, the Word of God tells us that the original intention of the Law was to expose sin rather than to establish our own righteousness.

"Be it known unto you therefore, brethren, that through this man [the Lord Jesus] is proclaimed unto you remission of sins; and by Him every one that believeth is justified from all things, from which ye could not be justified by the law of Moses." (Acts 13:38-39) So it is clear. We cannot be justified by our own works. We have committed so many sins that the very memory of them causes us great sorrow in our hearts. Nevertheless, in spite of all our failures, the Lord Jesus is still trustworthy. By believing in Him, our sins are forgiven; by trusting in Him, we are justified. The salvation of the Lord is indeed great!

As said before, the only condition for God's gift of salvation is faith. This faith is to believe in the Word of God. What is the Word of God?

1) *"And the Word became flesh and dwelt among us, and we beheld His glory, the glory as of the only begotten of the Father, full of grace and truth."* (John 1:14)

2) *"I am the way, the truth, and the life. No one can come to the Father except through Me."* (John 14:60)

3) *"For by grace you have been saved through faith, and that not of yourselves; it is the gift of God, not of works, lest anyone should boast."* (Ephesians 2:8, 9)

4) *"Anyone who believes and is baptized will be saved. But anyone who refuses to believe will be condemned."* (Matthew 28:16)

5) *"I assure you, anyone who believes in Me already has eternal life."* (John 6:47)

6) *"...He who has the Son has the life; he who does not have the Son of God does not have the life. I have written these things to you that you may know that you have eternal life, to you who believe into the name of the Son of God."* (1 John 5:12-13)

7) *"I am the resurrection and the life; he who believes in me, even if he should die, shall live."* (John 11:25)

8) *"Therefore I said to you that you will die in your sins; for unless you believe that "I Am," you will die in you sins."* (John 8:24)
9) *"The blood of Jesus His Son cleanses us from every sin." (*1John 1:7)
10) *"And as Moses lifted up the serpent in the wilderness, even so must the Son of Man be lifted up, that whoever believes in Him should not perish, but have eternal life."* (John 3:14-15)
11) *"For God so loved the world that He gave His only begotten Son, that everyone who believes on Him may not perish, but have eternal life."* (John 3:16)
12) *"He who believes in the Son has everlasting life; and he who does not believe in the Son shall not see life, but the wrath of God abides on him."* (John 3:36)
13) *"There is therefore now no condemnation to those who are in Christ Jesus...."* (Romans 8:1)
14) *"Therefore whoever confesses Me before men, him I will also confess before My Father who is in heaven."* (Matthew 10:32)

The Bible places great emphasis on the work of Christ. It tells us that God accepts us because of the work of Christ ("His precious blood"), not because of our own works. Each time we come before God it is based on what Christ is before God, not on what we are before Him. God esteems Christ highly, not us. Even if we could do better than Peter, John, and Paul, we would still only come before God because of Christ. It is Christ who brings us before God, not our own good works.

I trust that we have made it clear that we come before God by what Christ has accomplished. God does not accept any other sacrifice for sin other than the death of Jesus Christ His Son on the Cross. (Hebrews 10:26-27) If someone deliberately rejects the sacrifice of Jesus after clearly understanding the Good News teaching about it, then there is no way for that person to be saved. Acts 4:12 says, *"There is salvation in no one else! There is no name in all of heaven for people to call on to save them."*

The salvation of the Lord Jesus is now accomplished. Whoever is willing to believe in His name – that is, whoever is willing to accept Him as the Son of God and His sub-stitutionary death on the Cross for us – will become a child of God. Those who are not willing are "...*the tares which are the sons of the evil one ... which at the consummation of the age ... are collected and burned up with fire."* (Matthew 13:38-40)

Can you see how important this truth is? Eternal life or eternal death fully depends on whether or not man will accept God's salvation! There is only one condition for becoming the Sons of God, and that is to believe, to receive the Lord Jesus as Savior. Only by trusting in Him can one become a son of God. It is not of works, not of conduct, not of oneself, but – as we said earlier – of *faith.*

Now redemption is totally accomplished! Salvation leaves nothing for you to do to have eternal life, since the Lord has completed this for you.

1) He has paid the full price that you may be freely saved without any cost.
2) He descended from Heaven that you might ascend there.
3) He suffered the enmity of sinners so that you might receive the acceptance of God.
4) He was temporarily forsaken by the Father that you might be eternally welcomed by the Father.
5) He became poor that you might be rich.
6) He died on the Cross that you might live in Heaven.

With respect to the assurance of salvation, how can we know who has eternal life and is saved? Remember we told you that in the New Testament there are at least 150 places wherein the writers declare that he who believes has eternal life, has life, is not judged, or is saved. John 3:16, tells us that God loves us beyond our human comprehension. God has so loved the world that He has given His beloved and only begotten Son Jesus, who has died for sinners and has accomplished the work of redemption! So that now, *"...whosoever believeth on Him should not perish but have eternal life."*

This precious verse raises three points: a great fact, a great condition, and a great consequence.

1) The great fact is that God sent Jesus to atone for men's sins as the Savior of the world.

2) The great condition is what every man ought to do – which is to say – to believe.

3) The great consequence is actually so good, it is beyond human thought: *whoever believes shall not perish but have eternal life*. There is no other fact in the whole world greater or more real than this!

The great condition or demand is now put before every person for him to fulfill – to believe in the fact of what God has done and accomplished. That is the one and only condition. The great fact is done by God but the great condition is fulfilled by men. And with the great consequence of not perishing but having eternal life, a person is in possession of salvation.

Now, once the Lord has said this in His Word, can anyone possibly think that if any person believes, he or she will nonetheless perish? This would make God unjust, which He is not, for He is the God of righteousness. Therefore the Word of God stands sure: whoever believes in Jesus shall not perish but have eternal life.

Consider also John 6:47: *"Verily, verily, I say unto you, He that believeth on me hath everlasting life."* And God's Word never changes. This Scripture says it plainly, and by itself is enough to solve the problem of salvation. Faith is not expectation. It neither waits for the future (we do not need to die first to know that we are going to Heaven) nor requires work of any sort.

If you have not yet accepted the Lord Jesus as your Savior and have not become a child of God through Him, you are still of Adam and of the devil. Adam sinned, begetting children in his own sinful image (Genesis 5:1-3). You are the direct descendant of Adam; apart from regeneration, there is no other way for you to become a child of God. Make no mistake – hell is real! Three times Jesus speaks of hell in Mark 9:44, 46, 48 as being a place of terrible torment where *"Their worm does not die, And the fire is not quenched."*

Because of Adam, our spirits are dead even though our body is alive. But after we believe in the Lord Jesus, our spirits unite with the Holy Spirit within us to become our life. This is what the Bible calls being "reborn" in spiritual rebirth. Christ, by means of the Holy Spirit, now dwells within believers. This is the most important truth of the Gospel!

Don't believe that just because you think you are "better than others" that you are not a child of the devil!

You must understand that God has only one kind of children: those who have been redeemed by the Lord Jesus through believing in Him.

Only they are the children of God.

God does not save anyone else.

Jesus made it clear: *"I am the way, the truth, and the life. No one comes to the Father except through Me."* (John 14:6)

Is there any love greater than this? Please sinner, do not harden your heart. Wait no longer! Come now! The Lord still extends hope to you.

Remember the title of this book? I repeat. "You'd better believe it!" Where you spend eternity depends upon it!

Please do not wait to make the decision to believe in Him. Tomorrow may be too late.